LIVING BLACK HISTORY

Also by MANNING MARABLE

African and Caribbean Politics:
From Kwame Nkrumah to the Grenada Revolution

The Autobiography of Medgar Evers:
A Hero's Life and Legacy Revealed
Through His Writings, Letters, and Speeches
(coeditor with Myrlie Evers-Williams)

Beyond Black and White:
Transforming African American Politics

Black American Politics:
From the Washington Marches to Jesse Jackson

Black Leadership:
Four Great American Leaders and the
Struggle for Civil Rights

Black Liberation in Conservative America:
Essays on Race, Politics, and Society

Blackwater:
Historical Studies in Race,
Class Consciousness, and Revolution

The Crisis of Color and Democracy:
Essays on Race, Class, and Power

Dispatches from the Ivory Tower:
Intellectuals Confront the African American Experience
(editor)

Freedom:
A Photographic History of the
African American Freedom Struggle
(coauthor with Leith Mullings)

Freedom on My Mind:
The Columbia Documentary History of the
African American Experience
(editor)

From the Grassroots:
Essays Toward Afro-American Liberation

The Great Wells of Democracy:
The Meaning of Race in American Life

How Capitalism Underdeveloped Black America: Problems
in Race, Political Economy, and Society

Let Nobody Turn Us Around:
Voices of Resistance, Reform, and Renewal
(coeditor with Leith Mullings)

The New Black Renaissance:
The *Souls* Anthology of Critical African-American Studies
(editor)

Race, Reform, and Rebellion:
The Second Reconstruction in Black America, 1945–1990

Speaking Truth to Power:
Essays on Race, Radicalism, and Resistance

W. E. B. Du Bois: Black Radical Democrat

LIVING BLACK HISTORY

How Reimagining the African-American Past Can Remake America's Racial Future

MANNING MARABLE

BASIC
CIVITAS
BOOKS

A Member of the Perseus Books Group
New York

Designed by Trish Wilkinson
Set in 11.5-point Sabon by the Perseus Books Group

Library of Congress Cataloging-in-Publication Data
Marable, Manning, 1950-
    Living Black history : how reimagining the African-American past
can remake America's racial future / Manning Marable.
        p.   cm.
    Includes bibliographical references and index.
    ISBN-13: 978-0-465-04389-7 (hardcover)
    ISBN-10: 0-465-04389-5 (hardcover)
    1. African Americans—Historiography. 2. African Americans—
History—Philosophy. 3. African Americans—Intellectual life.
4. African Americans—Civil rights. 5. Social justice—United States.
6. United States—Race relations. I. Title.
E184.65.M37 2005
973'.0496073—dc22   2005021166

06 07 08 / 10 9 8 7 6 5 4 3 2

The 2004 W. E. B. Du Bois Lectures at Harvard University, and the added essays here, were inspired by three great icons of the black freedom struggle:

Ossie Davis
Myrlie Evers-Williams
Robert L. Carter

Their courageous legacies endure—past, present, and future.

Contents

Preface and Acknowledgments

". . . God of our weary years,
God of our silent tears,
Thou who has brought us thus far on the way;
Thou who has by Thy might,
Led us into the light,
Keep us forever in the path, we pray.
Lest our feet stray from the places,
Our God, where we met Thee;
Lest, our hearts drunk with
The wine of the world, we forget Thee;
Shadowed beneath thy hand, may we forever stand.
True to our God, true to our native land."
— "LIFT EV'RY VOICE AND SING", 1900.
(LYRICS BY JAMES WELDON JOHNSON;
MUSIC BY J. ROSAMOND JOHNSON)

LIVING BLACK HISTORY WAS INSPIRED BY TWO EVENTS, involving two icons of twentieth-century black history. In March 2003, Myrlie Evers-Williams, the former National

Chairman of the NAACP and the widow of martyred civil rights leader Medgar Evers, contacted me to deliver the first honorary "Medgar Evers Lecture" in Jackson, Mississippi. It was the fortieth anniversary of Evers's brutal assassination in front of his Jackson home, and the occasion would be marked by a series of public events including a long-overdue recognition by both the governor and the state legislature of Mississippi.

As I began researching in preparation for the lecture, I was struck by the absence of any detailed literature on this pivotal figure in African-American history. While no scholarly biography existed of Medgar Evers there were several detailed studies of his assassin, Byron de la Beckwith. Even in the 1996 Hollywood film *Ghosts of Mississippi,* which depicts Evers's assassination and Myrlie's thirty-year crusade to bring her late husband's killer to justice, Evers himself is only present as a ghost. Viewers are given absolutely no historical background as to Evers's courageous battle to destroy the particularly brutal brand of Jim Crow racism that flourished in Mississippi for so long. I soon became convinced of the urgency in preserving Evers's legacy: His speeches, writings, and other important documents pertaining to his life and politics/activism had to be published and available for future generations.

I traveled again to Mississippi in 2004 and began a close friendship with Myrlie. When Myrlie invited me to visit her former home, I thought I was prepared for what would surely be an emotional experience. Yet no amount of historical study or documentary knowledge could have truly prepared me for the tangible power of past tragedy held in that physical place. Myrlie and I stood in the driveway of their home, where the assassin's bullet had struck Medgar in the back. Kneeling, she softly explained that for months following Medgar's murder she would go outside in the dark of the night and vigorously attempt to scrub the bloodstains off the driveway. No matter how hard she scrubbed, no matter how many sleepless nights she spent trying, Medgar's bloodstains would not come clean. Her plaintive words were almost apologetic: She had been unable to wipe clean a stain that had left her without a loving husband and her children without a father. I was so overwhelmed I could barely keep from weeping aloud.

Walking into her modest home, Myrlie explained how the bullet that had killed Medgar ripped through his upper body, then crashed through the living room front window, through a wall, and into the small kitchen. It ricocheted off the refrigerator—the bullet's scar is still visible—and came to rest on the kitchen countertop next to a watermelon. We then walked to the master bedroom. Medgar usually slept on the right side of their bed, next to the windows. He always kept a loaded gun next to his nightstand. Myrlie slept on the left, and kept her own gun nearby as well. Facing almost constant threats for nearly a decade—while investigating the murders and lynchings of Mississippi blacks such as Emmett Till—they were dedicated to the struggle for black freedom. They lived their lives with the knowledge that death was ultimately inevitable, if not imminent. Myrlie told me that the day before Medgar's murder she had spent the afternoon starching and ironing about a dozen of her husband's white dress shirts. Medgar happened to come home early that day, and he saw Myrlie busily ironing his shirts. "Aren't you going to thank me for taking care of your shirts?" she asked her husband. Medgar's voice lowered. "I'm not going to be needing them."

What we, as Americans, owe Medgar and Myrlie Evers can scarcely be put into words. To sacrifice everything—personal safety, income, and life itself—for the cause of democracy and equal justice is monumental. Yet days following Medgar's death, the grief-stricken office staff at the Jackson NAACP headquarters unthinkingly packed up roughly twenty drawers of files documenting his tireless labors as the state's first field secretary. Medgar's files were then dumped into the garbage, disappearing for all time from recorded history. About four boxes of personal items, papers, and memorabilia were retained and dropped off at the family's residence. A well-meaning neighbor, thinking that the boxes in the family's carport were trash, took them to the front curb to be picked up by the sanitation truck. One of those boxes was taken by garbage collectors; fortunately for black history, the others were not.

The near-disappearance of Medgar Evers from the pages of American history illustrates just how fragile our heritage has become. Too often the study of history is an exercise in nostalgia or political myth-making rather than an honest interaction with the raw materials of the past. Understanding how Medgar employed tactics to energize and mobilize thousands of oppressed rural black folks to shake off their bondage and to boldly demand equal rights can provide practical examples of how a new generation of African

Americans and other minorities might challenge racism today. Preserving the past creates a living legacy that can help shape the future.

The second incident that inspired the writing of *Living Black History* involves the legacy of Trinidadian Marxist intellectual C. L. R. James. With the sole exception of W. E. B. Du Bois, James had the greatest impact on my own intellectual development. For half a century he personified the ideal of the "activist intellectual" by writing fearless indictments of colonialism and racism in the Caribbean, Africa, Europe, and the United States. In 1987, it was my great privilege to meet and talk at length one afternoon with "Nello," as he was widely known, in his tiny flat in the Brixton section of London. Through a series of complicated circumstances, James's archives, consisting of priceless correspondence, manuscripts, and handwritten texts, were stored in Manhattan's Upper West Side, not far from Columbia University. James Murray, a dedicated research assistant to James, had relocated the archive there and had established it as the C. L. R. James Center. In 2002 I met with Murray, and that fall semester I offered him a visiting professorship in African-American studies at Columbia, where he taught a James seminar.

In 2003 Murray died suddenly. Two groups of C. L. R. James's associates, one based in London and the other aligned with the late Murray primarily in the United States, disputed the ownership of the archive's physical and intellectual property. Prior to his death, Murray had been in negotiations with my colleagues at Columbia's

Rare Book and Manuscript Library for the acquisition of the James archive. I had drawn up an ambitious plan to complement the archive. The plan included an online search engine to help scholars with their research, as well as public conferences and exhibitions of James's papers to celebrate his political and intellectual accomplishments. We also would have established educational links between Columbia and the University of the West Indies. All of this would have culminated with the Internet publication of many of James's manuscripts and correspondence.

Unfortunately, since James had failed to outline a clear plan for preserving and making accessible the bulk of his scholarship, his closest friends and associates found it impossible to reach a compromise for ensuring his intellectual legacy. The legal dispute tied up James's archives completely. Young doctoral and master's degree students seeking to gain access to James's archives for research purposes have been deeply disappointed to learn that the papers are now boxed and sealed in the deep recesses of Columbia University's Butler Library. Once again, part of our black heritage is lost.

When the W. E. B. Du Bois Institute and the African-American Studies Department at Harvard University, headed by my friend Henry Louis Gates Jr., graciously invited me to deliver its prestigious 2004 W. E. B. Du Bois Lectures, I found myself thinking about my experiences with Myrlie and the legal dispute over C. L. R. James's papers. I decided to use the lectures to engage the problems of how black history can be both lost and sustained, as well as the connection between historical consciousness and political and social change. In early 2004 I drafted three lectures on these themes and I delivered them at Harvard University that April: "Living Black History: Black Consciousness, Place, and America's Master Narrative"; "Malcolm X's Life-After-Death: The Dispossession of a Legacy"; and "The Unfulfilled Promise of *Brown*: From Desegregation to Global Racial Justice." With significant modifications and revisions, these lectures appear here as Chapters 1, 4, and 5. Chapter 2, "Mapping Black Political Culture: Leadership, Intellectuals, and Resistance," was first drafted in May 2004 and evolved into its current form by June 2005. Chapter 3, "Resurrecting the Radical Du Bois," actually began as a short essay in late 2003 and evolved into a lecture delivered at the opening plenary of the American Sociological Convention in San Francisco in August 2004. Its current form was completed in July 2005. Greatly revised versions of parts of Chapter 3 appeared as "Celebrating *Souls*: Deconstructing the Du Boisian Legacy" in W. E. B. Du Bois, *The Souls of Black Folk*, 100th Anniversary Edition (Boulder: Paradigm Publishers, 2004) and "Introduction," in Manning Marable, *W. E. B. Du Bois: Black Radical Democrat*, Revised Edition (Boulder: Paradigm Publishers, 2005). Part of Chapter 4 appeared, in a slightly different version, as "Rediscovering Malcolm's Life," in my journal, *Souls*, vol. 7, no. 1 (winter 2005). Part of Chapter 5 was published as "The Promise of *Brown*: Desegregation, Affirmative Action and the Struggle for Racial Equality," *Negro Educational Review*, vol. 56, no. 1 (January 2005), and "Beyond Brown: The Revolution in Black Studies," *Black Scholar*, vol. 35, no. 2 (Summer 2005).

Living Black History is an intellectual and political intervention for all Americans, but particularly those of us of African descent. The artifacts, memorabilia, and archives of the great black forerunners in the fight for freedom and democracy are seriously endangered, and precious little is being done about it. Priceless records, films, photographs, and crucial documents that reveal the inner stories of remarkable African-American women and men are rapidly being destroyed—whether through neglect, physical deterioration, or legal disputes which keep them from being properly archived and preserved. Frequently the destruction of black heritage is economically motivated. Private letters and memorabilia of black icons like Malcolm X are hoarded by private collectors, and then sold to the highest bidder, disappearing from public access.

Sometimes the destruction of black heritage is ideological, as in the cases of the families of Martin Luther King Jr. and of Malcolm X and Dr. Betty Shabazz. The Kings' goal is to "freeze" Martin on the steps of the Lincoln Memorial, delivering his "I Have a Dream" address, thus isolating him from his 1967–1968 radical antiwar, pro–Poor Peoples' March phase. The Shabazzes prefer to focus on Malcolm's youthful prepolitical period and his final year outside the Nation of Islam, while minimizing the profound significance of his devotion to Elijah Muhammad and his extensive involvement and identification with the conservative black nationalist tenets of the Nation of Islam.

For me, being true to black history, for me, means accepting and interpreting its totality. The historian's task is to preserve everything that has substantive significance, and to resist the temptation of imposing our own latter-day perceptions on the content of our subjects. We can best honor the sacrifices of those African Americans who died to achieve freedom by recording and interpreting accurately what they actually said and did, and then making that information available to the widest possible public audience through texts, films, the Internet, and multimedia resources.

Living Black History also examines the role of the activist-intellectual in the making of modern black history. I have chosen to focus on three individuals: W. E. B. Du Bois, preeminent black intellectual of the twentieth century; Malcolm X (El Hajj Malik El Shabazz), fiery black nationalist and later human rights advocate; and NAACP General Counsel Robert L. Carter. In the cases of Du Bois and Malcolm X, there has been a collective theft of the true content of their radical ideas and revolutionary politics in different ways. In Carter's case, most African Americans have failed to appreciate that the best way to honor the tremendous legal achievement of *Brown v. Board of Education* that he helped to engineer is to critique its successes and failures, and to transcend its limitations by pursuing a new political and legal strategy to challenge structural racism as it presently exists.

A half century ago, Du Bois, Malcolm X, and Carter, in very different ways, all struggled to overthrow the immoral regime of Jim Crow segregation and the destructive psychological sense of dependency and inferiority it engendered among their people. The challenges today are different: Instead of legal segregation, we are confronted internationally with a growing "global apartheid," and domestically with a "color-blind racism." Both are defined by mass unemployment, mass incarceration, and mass disfranchisement. This "New Racial Domain" of color-blind racism can be undermined, in part, by harnessing the living power of black heritage and our narratives of resistance. Preserving our proud past and presenting with integrity the stories of these extraordinary women and men helps us to imagine new futures, and to use history as a critical force for change. In this manner, we may "forever stand, true to our God, true to our native land."

Reconstructing the hidden, fragmented past of African Americans can be accomplished with a multidisciplinary methodology employing the tools of oral history, photography, film, ethnography, and multimedia digital technology, an approach I call "living history." The larger civic objective of living history projects is to stimulate a new kind of historically grounded conversation about race and the destructive processes of racialization. America is a nation that continues to evade and obscure from its own citizens the central drama of its development—the glaring contradiction of structural inequality that was justified by the color of one's skin.

Blacks acquired and came to believe deeply in the democratic discourse to which whites claimed an allegiance. They bitterly learned, however, that the constitutional guarantees and the administration of laws protecting individual rights were not extended to them. In response, they established organizations and institutions that both preserved their unique cultural gifts, families, and heritage and also asserted their rights to be treated as equals. They also struggled for what historians describe as "self-determination"—the ability to decide collectively for themselves what the future development of their group should be, and what new institutional arrangements would be necessary to achieve those ends.

A new civic conversation about race in America's historical development requires the unearthing of physical sites of atrocities, from the Jackson, Mississippi, home of Medgar Evers, to Manhattan's Audubon Ballroom, where Malcolm X was assassinated. That honest conversation would include a discussion about the possible role of governmental and public agencies in creating the conditions that culminated in the deaths of prominent African Americans, as well as thousands of others whose lives went unrecorded and forgotten. The process of frank reevaluation of a shared past of suffering and struggle may prompt a rededication to enduring democratic values and policies, which will bring at long last all elements of our fragmented nation into a common civic project.

Many people assisted in the development of *Living Black History*. My graduate research assistants Elizabeth Mazucci, Mio Matsumoto, and Zaheer Ali all contributed extensively in tracking down invaluable information. Professor Farah Jasmine Griffin, the Director of Columbia University's Institute for Research in African-American Studies, generously granted me leave time in 2004 to complete research on both this book and *The Autobiography of Medgar Evers* (New York: Basic Civitas, 2005). The Institute's outstanding staff, especially Shawn Mendoza,

Glenda Walker, and Sharon Harris, was always especially helpful. Sara Crafts, my typist–research assistant, expertly processed the entire manuscript through its many versions and helped keep the entire project on track and on time. My gifted, sympathetic editors at Basic *Civitas*, Elizabeth Maguire and Chris Greenberg, made key suggestions for strengthening and revising the final text, greatly improving the book. Chris devoted much time and effort in helping me to translate the mundane information drawn from historical research into a style and language that would be accessible to a general audience, a challenge that many historians unfortunately fail to address.

Finally, the debt I can never fully repay is to Leith Mullings, a great intellectual-activist in the true radical tradition of W. E. B. Du Bois. Leith is admittedly the intellectual collaborator on most of my best ideas. She will always be "my bright and morning star."

Manning Marable
July 31, 2005

Living Black History

Black Consciousness, Place, and
America's Master Narrative

> History is a form within which we fight, and many have
> fought before us. Nor are we alone when we fight there.
> For the past is not dead, inert, confining; it carries signs
> and evidences also of creative resources which can sustain
> the present and prefigure possibility.
> —EDWARD THOMPSON

WE ALL "LIVE HISTORY" EVERY DAY. BUT HISTORY IS
more than the construction of collective experiences, or the
knowledge drawn from carefully catalogued artifacts from
the past. History is also the architecture of a people's memory, framed by our shared rituals, traditions, and notions
of common sense. It can be a ragged bundle of hopes, especially for those who have been relegated beyond society's
brutal boundaries.

For the majority of Americans, "American history" is a
narrative about an inevitable series of conquests: over indig-
enous people, over frontiers, over boundaries and borders,

over vast stretches of geography, and even over space itself. Embedded in that conquest is a set of ideas about individual liberty, the ownership of private property, and certain restrictions on the authority and power of the central government over personal activity. The history that is generally codified in classroom textbooks and sets the boundaries of civic discourse emphasizes the character of the American experience as both "exceptional" and "unique," but also "universal," in the sense that our history's underlying core democratic values can be transported and adopted by other peoples in distant lands, thereby enhancing the quality of their lives. To become "American" is to accept the legitimacy of this master narrative.

Unfortunately, there is considerable historical evidence—for example, Native American artifacts, the burial ground of enslaved Africans next to Wall Street, and remnants of internment camps formerly holding Japanese Americans during World War II—that undermines the coherence and legitimacy of that master narrative of American history. Consensus and intragroup cooperation, rather than conflict, are deliberately emphasized, with the objective of assimilating opposing interests and factions into a pluralistic, harmonious whole—*e pluribus unum*. However, in a society historically organized around structural racism, this task is, at best, difficult because it demands the selective suppression of historical evidence itself.

This suppression can occur in small ways, such as the National Park Service's previous description of the sites of slave shanties behind George Washington's Mount Vernon estate and Thomas Jefferson's Monticello as "servants' quarters." Or, in the case of the all-black neighborhood of Rosewood, Florida, it can occur on an almost unbelievably large scale. In the aftermath of the murderous mass assault by whites against blacks in January 1923, the perpetrating whites proceeded with the physical elimination of any evidence that an African-American community once existed there at all. There is too often a deliberate distancing of whites from the common hidden history they actually share with black people.

The darkest aspects of American history have often been hidden from plain view because of the power of the past—or at least the power of the popularly perceived past—to shape the realities of our daily lives. Ignorance of our shared history sustains our parallel racial universes. On the outskirts of Jerusalem (now Courtland), Virginia, in late August of 1831, a band of slave rebels led by charismatic preacher Nat Turner began butchering white men, women, and children. Within thirty-six hours about sixty white slaveholders and their family members had been killed. The white authorities responded with overwhelming force, rounding up the rebels along with over one hundred African Americans who had not been involved in the insurrection. As many as two hundred blacks were burned alive, beheaded, and/or lynched. Turner himself was captured and hung on November 11, 1831. His corpse was decapitated, and strips of his skin were removed and sewn into souvenir purses. The remnants of his body were buried in an unmarked grave near a railroad track.

Today, six of the twenty-nine slave-owners' houses that Turner and his followers attacked still stand. One current owner proudly displays a bullet hole left from the 1831 rebellion. Aside from a few bullet holes, few signposts bear witness to these events. The most visible, and literal, representation of the uprising is "Blackhead Signpost Road," so named because an African-American slave rebel's severed head had been mounted high on a stake along the country road. The continued existence (until recently) of "Blackhead Signpost Road" into the twenty-first century is an indication that white Americans are still taught to believe that "being white" means never having to say they are sorry.

For almost two centuries, white America has had difficulty explaining the reasons for Nat Turner's infamous revolt, which unleashed such violence against "innocent" whites. In the aftermath of the uprising, the *New York Morning Courier and Enquirer* in 1831 questioned why "mistresses famed for their kindness—virgins renowned for their beauty and little helpless lisping infants in the cradle, were in short, hewed down with axes, butchered with knives, and had their brains dashed out . . . by those fiends in human form." But from the terrain of black consciousness, a different set of questions emerges, all predicated on the right of the oppressed to use any means at their disposal to overturn the forces of domination against them. To W. E. B. Du Bois, for instance, Nat Turner was "the preacher revolutionist" who believed he "was to lead the liberation movement and that the first should be last and the last first." For actor Ossie Davis, Turner represented "our secret weapon, our ace in the hole, our private consciousness on manhood." For these African Americans, Turner's actions required no apologies.

A few miles from the site of the Turner uprising is another marker of the hidden history of racial injustice. In the 1950s, blacks in Farmville, Virginia, mobilized to demand the desegregation of their public schools. Whites responded with the same fervor they exhibited in resisting Nat Turner: They immediately closed the public schools for years. Whites set up private academies for their children while a "lost generation" of blacks lacked access to quality secondary education and thus were penalized for life. When desegregation was finally enforced in the fall of 1964, only eight whites showed up at the public school buldings to attend classes with fifteen hundred blacks. It took nearly forty years, until 2003, for the Virginia legislature to pass a resolution admitting its "profound regret" for the closing of Farmville's public schools. There was, however, no compensation given to the "lost generation" or their descendants.

The physical sites of Nat Turner's uprising and the public school buildings in Farmville, Virginia, are important because our national memory is closely linked with geography, physical spaces, and material culture. When African Americans attempt to reconstruct narratives told by their great-grandparents and grandparents, the physical sites of these narratives invoke the smells, sounds, tastes, and cultural textures of black daily life that may no longer exist. They provide a firm grounding from which a meaningful interpretation becomes possible. This is particularly the case with sites marking a horrific event that represents a larger social reality, such as structural racism.

In the Bronx, the residence of Amadou Diallo—a West African immigrant killed on February 4, 1999, by four plainclothes officers of New York City's Street Crimes Unit, who shot at him forty-one times and struck him with nineteen bullets—has become an impromptu site of community mourning, grief, and political anger about police brutality. Flowers are left in the vestibule and outside the building on the anniversary of his death. For most Americans the site of President John F. Kennedy's assassination in Dallas, Texas, is officially considered "hallowed ground," whereas the Audubon Ballroom in Manhattan, where Malcolm X was brutally murdered on February 21, 1965, and the Bronx site of Diallo's killing are not.

Frequently American history's places or sites of racist tragedies are difficult if not impossible to mark for memorialization. In 1765, for example, Nicholas Brown Sr., a wealthy Rhode Island merchant, commissioned the ship *Sally* to trade cargoes of rum and other manufactured goods to the west coast of Africa for the purchase of enslaved Africans. The captain of the slave vessel was under orders to carry *Sally*'s human cargo to Barbados, where the bulk of Africans were to be sold. Four Africans, each approximately fifteen years old, were to be transported back to Rhode Island, where they were to become the personal household slaves of the Brown family.

The initial phase of *Sally*'s voyage to West Africa went according to plan, but things quickly fell apart when the ship started to cross the Atlantic. Africans who were brought up on deck hurled themselves into the ocean, deliberately choosing death rather than descending back below deck. Scores of slaves began dying from fever, lack of food, and unsanitary conditions. One determined African woman managed to hang herself below deck to protest her captivity. When one party of slaves was brought up on deck, they attempted to physically overpower the white crewmen: Eight slaves were shot and killed. By the time *Sally* reached the West Indies, over one hundred of the original one hundred sixty-seven enslaved Africans had died.

There is no historical marker for the victims of *Sally*'s journey, either on some remote island in the South Atlantic or in Rhode Island. But a memorial to honor Brown and his even more successful son, Nicholas Brown Jr., a prominent banker and merchant, was subsequently constructed. Nicholas Brown Sr.'s brother, John Brown, continued to purchase and transport hundreds of slaves into the Caribbean and the United States during and after the American Revolution. There is some evidence that unpaid black labor was used by the Brown family at its ironworks factory in Massachusetts, and in its candle factory located in Providence. The Browns were devoted to the cause of American independence, and volunteered their ships to transport crucial supplies to General George Washington's beleaguered troops. But these same ships were also used to bring African slaves to the United States against their will. None of these ironies of history troubled the founding fathers of Rhode Island College, renamed Brown University in 1804 to honor the chief benefactors of that academic institution.

Brown University's institutional connections with the transatlantic slave trade and slavery were hardly unique. Many of America's oldest and most prestigious universities, banks, and corporations have similar links. At Yale University, eight of the twelve named residential colleges on campus are named in honor of slaveholders. A significant landmark on Yale's campus, Livingston Gateway, was named to honor early college benefactor Philip Livingston, one of "the biggest slave traders in the American colonies." Columbia University has a similar history. Founded in 1754 as George II's "King's College" on the island of Manhattan, the school sought the patronage of affluent merchants, many of whom were directly involved in slave trading, or who materially profited from the unpaid labor of African Americans.

One of Columbia's most revered founding fathers was William Alexander, Lord Stirling, a governor of King's College from 1763 to 1782. In 1748, Alexander and a business partner, John Stevens, commissioned a ship to Africa, bringing back to New York City's harbor a cargo of slaves for sale. From the profits of this initial venture, Alexander purchased two slave ships of his own, according to archivist Marilyn H. Pettit, "working in business-like fashion until unprofitability set in." Enslaved African Americans worked at Lord Stirling's "sumptuous estate at Basking Ridge, New Jersey, throughout the Revolutionary War." Brockholst Livingston, Columbia College trustee from 1787 until 1823, who also served as treasurer and chair of the college's board of trustees from 1816 to 1823, owned slaves at least until

1817. Columbia's eighth president, William Alexander Duer, serving from 1829 to 1842, was the grandson of both Alexander and John Duer, who made his fortune from slave plantations in Antigua and Dominica. At the same time, there were early prominent alumni of Columbia, such as Alexander Hamilton, who vigorously opposed the slave trade and slavery's expansion.

The recent national debate over "reparations," prompted by the 2000 publication of Randall Robinson's brilliant and provocative book, *The Debt*, led a number of state and local governments to consider enacting laws to force corporations to disclose any possible links they may have had with African-American slavery. After Chicago's city council passed a slavery disclosure law in 2002, for example, J. P. Morgan Chase revealed that two predecessor banks it once owned had accepted thirteen thousand enslaved African Americans owned by Louisiana slaveholders as collateral for a series of loans prior to the Civil War. When several of these loans defaulted, the banks seized possession of twelve hundred slaves and sold them. In January 2005, J. P. Morgan Chase issued a public "apology" and created "a $5 million scholarship for African Americans in Louisiana."

On June 1, 2005, the Wachovia Corporation, America's fourth largest bank, revealed that several of its predecessor institutions had also profited directly from slavery, and had permitted borrowers to use their enslaved African Americans as collateral for loans. A team of seven archivists and researchers employed by Wachovia devoted over 1,800 hours, sifting through two-hundred-year-old records housed at the Library of Congress and the Maryland Historical Society. Going over old bank ledgers, correspondence written by bank managers, and newspaper accounts, the story of corporate collusion with slave traders, slaveholding plantation owners, and businessmen began to unfold. In one instance, the Bank of Charleston, established in 1834, had taken possession of at least 529 slaves on defaulting mortgages and loans from white customers prior to the Civil War. The Bank of Charleston subsequently became part of the South Carolina National Corporation, which in 1991 merged into Wachovia. Another Wachovia predecessor bank, the Georgia Railroad and Banking Company, had bankrolled the construction of a Georgia railroad in 1833 using slave labor that involved at least 162 enslaved African Americans. Wachovia chairman and chief executive officer G. Kennedy Thompson declared to the media: "I apologize to all Americans, and especially to African Americans and people of African descent. . . . We know that we cannot change the past, and we can't make up for the wrongs of slavery, but we can learn from our past and begin a stronger dialogue about slavery and the experience of African Americans in our country."

In 2000, California became the first state to demand that insurance companies doing business there disclose information regarding policies they had issued years before involving slavery. On March 1, 2005, the Richmond, California, City Council adopted an ordinance mandating that its $150 million pension and city investment funds divest from financial institutions that previously profited from slavery. A similar debate for slavery divestment has erupted within the California Employees' Retirement System, the nation's largest public pension system.

The public pressure on corporations and financial institutions to reveal their links to both slavery and Jim Crow segregation policies has prompted several to make unprecedented admissions concerning both past and present discriminatory practices. One interesting example is provided by Eastman Kodak. In 1999, the Rochester, New York, chapter of the NAACP confronted Eastman Kodak's senior management about allegations of racial discrimination it had received from its minority employees. Kodak investigated the charges and admitted that discrimination was widespread throughout the company. It responded by distributing approximately $13 million in "restitution checks and salary increases" by 2004, and promoted an undisclosed number of minorities to managerial positions. Kodak also evaluated eight hundred employees, assessing their "ability to manage in a diverse environment," and demoted or removed about two hundred people from managerial and supervisory positions. Such concessions, while commendable, were not sufficient for many African-American Kodak employees, who still perceived that blacks as a group continued to earn less than their white counterparts performing similar tasks. On July 30, 2004, a group of former and current Kodak employees sued the corporation in Federal District Court, charging Eastman Kodak with continued systematic discrimination against African Americans.

A few institutions have creatively attempted to atone for their racist pasts by removing embarrassing symbols or landmarks from their property that were connected with slavery or racial segregation. One example was the noble effort of Vanderbilt University in Nashville, Tennessee. In 1935, the "United Daughters of the Confederacy" donated $50,000 to Vanderbilt; it was used towards the construction of a new campus building named "Confederate Memorial Hall." Since African Americans were banned by race from attending Vanderbilt at that time, no one raised objections. By 2002, a racially integrated Vanderbilt, attempting to enhance its multicultural image, initiated legal measures to remove the word "confederate" engraved in stone above the building that is now used as a dormitory. In May 2005, a state court ruled against Vanderbilt, declaring that the word "confederate" had to remain, unless the university agreed to return to the United Daughters of the Confederacy the inflation-adjusted sum of its 1935 donation, which by 2005 amounted to $690,246. Vanderbilt conceded its legal defeat, and left the confederate landmark unchanged. However, on its campus maps and other university literature, the dormitory has now become "Memorial Hall."

Conservatives who in recent years had largely succeeded in dismantling affirmative action policies and race-sensitive college scholarships were dismayed by these numerous examples of historical introspection and candor about racism, both past and present. They perceived the reparations discourse as a nefarious Pandora's box, threatening to undermine the legitimacy of all types of institutions, private and public. When Brown University President Ruth J. Simmons, the first African-American president of an Ivy League institution, announced in March 2004 the establishment of a "Committee on Slavery and Justice" to engage in a two-year investigation of the university's ties to black servitude, conservative critics wasted little time in denouncing her bold initiative. Economist Thomas Sowell ruminated in the conservative periodical *Human Events*: "This is to be no academic exercise of scholarly research. There is obviously supposed to be a pot of gold at the end of this rainbow." For Sowell, Simmons was duplicitously engaging in the sordid business of "race hustling. It is being coy about race hustling. At least Al Sharpton and Jesse Jackson are up front."

What perturbed Sowell and other conservative ideologues was that despite largely winning the legal battle to dismantle affirmative action, they were in danger of losing the larger moral war for reinterpreting America's divided racial past. Any serious, historically grounded excavation of the history of almost any major U. S. institution established prior to the Civil Rights movement could potentially reveal a virtual nightmare of racist atrocities and exploitation, suggesting not merely apologies, but the large-scale transferal of wealth to the descendants of slaves—the African-American population—as compensation. Sowell's worst fears may have been realized when a University of Alabama law professor, Alfred L. Brophy, urged his university in March 2004 to "apologize for owning slaves before the Civil War and consider granting reparations to their descendants." Brophy's research had uncovered that African-American slaves had routinely labored at the early campus from 1831 up to 1865. Two of the University of Alabama's earliest presidents also owned slaves.

Against this growing mountain of historical documentation—the millions of African-American families forcibly separated through sale; the generations of black slaves coerced to build university buildings, courthouses, banks, and railroads without compensation; the nameless millions denied access to higher education, employment, and access to health care under the intolerable regime of Jim Crow segregation—why do the great masses of white Americans remain unmoved? For them, the white past by its nature is remote from the present; the black past reveals nothing but an abyss. To explore the dark unknown is to lose touch with reality. Linking the black past too closely with the present could compromise their future. I think most African Americans intuitively understand all this, and recognize that their moral claim on American institutions is inextricably bound to their past. For us, the past is not simply prologue; it is indelibly part of the fabric of our collective destiny.

Indeed this alternate understanding of history, even more than race or culture, is the most important quality that makes African Americans as a people different from other Americans. To most blacks, existence meant struggle: We could never afford to stand still. White Americans could afford to evade or deny the deep ironies and contradictions embedded in their racialized democracy; we could not. C. L. R. James clearly understood this, as he observed in 1970:

The black people in the United States are the most socially united group in the country; they all have one
unifying characteristic—they suffer from that historical development which has placed them in the role
of second class citizens. There is no other national
group which automatically constitutes one social
force with a unified outlook and the capacity to make
unified moves in politics and to respond to economic
problems. . . . It is from America's urban blacks that
many people all over the world have historically
gained a consciousness of the problems that black
people suffer and their attempts to overcome them.

An independent black consciousness arose around the
recognition that "race" was the fundamental contradiction within the politics of the American state. That is because, as Martin Luther King Jr. and Malcolm X both
completely understood, U.S. democracy was constructed
on a distinctively racial foundation. The nation's first law,
the 1790 Emigration Act, limited citizenship solely to
"free white persons." That helps to explain why most
Asians born in continental Asia could not legally become
U.S. citizens until 1952, and why the majority of black
voters could not cast ballots in a U.S. presidential election
until 1968.

It is a people's proximity to state power—most simply
embodied in the ability to vote—that decides how they
think about "living history" in the United States. Because
of the difficult circumstances of their lives, the oppressed

sometimes tend to celebrate myth over factual accuracy, romantic resistance over silent subordination. Not only can the proximate access to power affect the experience of an entire people, it can also alter how a group will remember its most dynamic figures. To my knowledge, very few black poets have written lyrics in praise of the heroic exploits of Booker T. Washington, Condoleezza Rice, or Clarence Thomas. By contrast, there are literally hundreds of powerful poems, plays, symphonies, and even an opera inspired by Malcolm X. Blacks even make critical distinctions about "authenticity" among their most celebrated and popular public figures. Several years ago in my Malcolm X seminar at Columbia, I asked the students about the critical differences between Dr. Martin Luther King Jr. and Malcolm X. One black student quickly responded that "Dr. Martin Luther King Jr. belongs to the world, but Malcolm X belongs to us."

Black consciousness was also formed in response to the omnipresent reality of racist violence that generations of African Americans experienced in their daily lives. Such violence usually assumed the character of social exclusion, stigmatization, and physical and psychological intimidation, from being forced to descend from the sidewalk when whites walked by, to being denied service at restaurants or restrooms during the period of Jim Crow segregation. Yet always beneath the surface of this racially stratified civic order was the constant fear of lynching, or vigilante violence outside the sanction of legal authorities and the courts. From 1882 to 1927, over 3,500 blacks were lynched in the United States, about 95 percent in the South. An unknown number of additional African Americans were killed, especially in rural and remote areas, where we have few means to reconstruct these crimes.

Most white Americans today have a dim recognition that lynchings of some African Americans unfortunately happened in the distant past in the United States. But few comprehend just how prevalent and popular these criminal acts were, or that thousands of whites—some of their grandparents and parents—eagerly participated in these atrocities. Of the thousands of well-documented cases of lynchings during the past century, two particularly stand out for me. In Omaha, Nebraska, on the evening of September 28, 1919, a white mob of five thousand surrounded and raided the county courthouse, where an African-American male was being held, charged with assaulting a white female. The black man was seized from the local authorities, then was publicly executed. His body was shot an estimated one thousand times. For good measure, the mutilated corpse was burned. Dozens of defiant, smiling white men, many wearing white shirts, neckties, and business suits, posed proudly around the charred corpse for souvenir photographs. In Marion, Indiana, on August 7, 1930, a massive white mob stormed the jail in the local county courthouse, seizing two incarcerated African-American teenagers, Thomas Shipp and Abram Smith, who had been accused of raping a white woman. Within less than an hour, a festive gathering of several thousand white women and men armed with baseball bats, crowbars, and guns beat and then lynched the two black boys. A photograph of the Marion lynching depicts smiling young adults, a pregnant woman, teenage girls, and a middle-aged man, pointing proudly to one of the dangling corpses.

A third young African American, a sixteen-year-old shoeshine boy named James Cameron, was also seized and beaten by the mob that night. Several men lifted Cameron up, and a noose was slipped around his neck. Just at that moment, a local white man in the crowd pushed forward and declared that young Cameron was innocent. Years later, on June 13, 2005, speaking at a U.S. Senate news conference, 91-year-old James Cameron recalled: "They took the rope off my neck, those hands that had been so rough and ready to kill or had already killed, they took the rope off my neck and they allowed me to start walking and stagger back to jail, which was just a half-block away." Cameron, the only known survivor of an attempted lynching, had come to the Capitol as part of an effort to obtain a formal apology from the Senate for its historic refusal to pass federal legislation outlawing lynching. For decades, Southern senators had filibustered legislative attempts to ratify antilynching legislation, denouncing such bills as an unnecessary interference with states' rights. Prompted by the emotional testimony of Cameron and the family members and descendants of lynching victims, the Senate finally issued an apology for lynching—the first time in United States history that Congress has acknowledged and expressed regret for historical crimes against African Americans—in a formal resolution. What was most significant, perhaps, was that only eighty-five of the one hundred U.S. senators had co-sponsored the resolution when it came up for a voice vote. The fifteen senators who did not initially co-sponsor the bill were Republicans. Belatedly, seven senators subsequently signed an oversized copy of the senate's antilynching resolution that was to be publicly displayed. The eight senators who still refused to concede an apology are Lamar Alexander (R-Tennessee); Thad Cochran (R-Mississippi), John Cornyn (R-Texas), Michael Enzi (R-Wyoming), Judd Gregg (R-New Hampshire), Trent Lott (R-Mississippi), John Sununu (R-New Hampshire), and Craig Thomas (R-Wyoming).

Why the steadfast refusal to acknowledge the forensic evidence and the obvious human pain and suffering inflicted not only on the victims of racist violence, but upon their descendants? Because, as in the previously cited cases of profiteering from slavery, the white American master narrative about the past is predicated on the recognition that *history itself* is a central site of collective experience for the articulation of power relations and social hierarchies within any society. Historical narratives—the stories we teach about past events—become frameworks for understanding the past and for interpreting its meaning for our own time and in our individual lives. In this way, history's lessons, enduring symbols (such as the United States flag—"Old Glory"), iconic personalities, and distinctive language all have practical and powerful consequences in shaping civic behavior and social consciousness. These elements of our shared history thus help to influence public policy and the future direction of subsequent events and decisions that have not yet occurred.

In a racist society—by this, I mean a society deeply stratified with "whiteness" defined at the top and "blackness" occupying the bottom rungs—the obliteration of the black past is absolutely essential to the preservation of white hegemony, or domination. Since "race" itself is a fraudulent concept, devoid of scientific reality, "racism" can only be rationalized and justified through the suppression of black counternarratives that challenge society's understanding about itself and its own past. Racism is perpetuated and reinforced by the "historical logic of whiteness," which repeatedly presents whites as the primary (and frequently sole) actors in the important decisions that have influenced the course of human events. This kind of history deliberately excludes blacks and other racialized groups from having the capacity to become actors in shaping major social outcomes. In this process of falsification, two elements are crucial: the suppression of evidence of black resistance, and the obscuring of any records of white crimes and exploitation committed against blacks as an oppressed group. In this manner, white Americans can more easily absolve themselves of the historical responsibility for the actions of their great-grandparents, grandparents, parents—and of themselves. Thus the destructive consequences of modern structural racism that can be easily measured by social scientists within contemporary U.S. society today can be said to have absolutely nothing to do with whites as a racial group. Denial of responsibility for racism permits the racial chasm to grow wider with each passing year.

Because mainstream white American history is still largely organized around the preservation of the "historical logic of whiteness," narrative gaps, strange silences, and lacunae of all kinds litter its interpretive landscape. These irregular gaps mark events that once revealed the true distance between America's rhetoric about democracy and freedom versus its reality. Everyday events that have occurred under a racist society, such as a lynching, or the unjust arrest and incarceration of an innocent black person, are denied historical significance or merit, and are therefore not mentioned in standard narratives about the past. Truly outrageous incidents of racial brutality that have involved hundreds and even thousands of people, such as the 1923 destruction of Rosewood, Florida, are simply erased from civic memory and the standard history books for decades. Thus, by the logic of whiteness, black Americans have nothing to complain about, because they have no collective history worth remembering.

So as a black historian, the question that came to me was, "How can the *authentic history* of black people be brought to life?" By "authentic" I mean a historical narrative in which blacks themselves are the principal actors, and that the story is told and explained largely from their own vantage point. The authentic narrative rejects out of hand the inferiority—biological, genetic, or cultural—of people of African descent to any other branches of the human family. How can we rediscover evidence of silent, unrecorded holocausts where no markers or monuments have ever been constructed to note what happened? How can official archives, the compiled and preserved documents of public officials, be better used to discern the slender threads of black resistance and group contestation? How can heavily redacted documents from the files of the Federal Bureau of Investigation and various police agencies be dissected to reveal fresh evidence of black suppression and resistance?

Conceptually, a method of historical investigation had to be developed, I concluded, that reduced the distance between the past, the present, and the future to effectively reconstruct these authentic narratives. This was particularly important because the vast majority of African Americans, as well as poor and working-class people's political organizations and protest movements, rarely leave behind substantial texts or well-preserved written records that end up in official archives and major libraries. Precious documents, transcripts of important speeches, and crucial manifestos written by African Americans, produced by generation after generation, have been largely scattered, destroyed, and lost. Any method for reconstructing the authentic black voice and past would require, I came to realize, a multidisciplinary approach, in which archival investigation at traditional institutions might play only a secondary role.

Once again, my theoretical point of departure for constructing what I began to term "living history" came from the extraordinary insights of C. L. R. James. In a remarkable 1970 essay, "Black People in the Urban Areas of the United States," James argued that the collective struggles of blacks could not achieve the goal of freedom without the remaking of the totality of American society.

> The [black] people who dominate the inner cities numerically cannot possibly work out a plan or have any program by which they can improve their own situation which does not take into consideration the city as a whole. . . . A new situation has arisen for the urban black, for thinking in terms of the whole city means that you are automatically thinking in terms of the state and from the state you find yourself facing the whole nation.

Social historians have said for decades that the resistance movements of the African-American community throughout its history, but especially dating from the Great Migration of the early twentieth century, have been the basic template for other American social protest movements. This is undeniably true, not only in the United States but for social movements throughout much of the modern world. The civil rights movement (historian Clayborne Carson and I, among others, strongly prefer the term "black freedom movement") created a successful model of popular resistance that helped spawn the women's rights movement, the gay and lesbian rights movement, the Chicano liberation struggle, and many other resistance movements. The Black Panthers directly inspired the Puerto Rican Young Lords Party, AIM (American Indian Movement), and even struggles among white American senior citizens calling themselves the Gray Panthers.

While few Americans, regardless of race, can recall the words or ideas expressed in a George W. Bush presidential address, few will ever forget the phrase "I Have a Dream," uttered by Martin on the steps of the Lincoln Memorial that hot August afternoon in 1963. Stamped deeply into public memory, it is now central to our understanding of what American democracy should be. Martin's language still resonates for us today, not simply because he was a moving and powerful orator, but because his words had real depth and social meaning to every American. He spoke about the everyday problems of African Americans while appealing to the institutionalized promises of American democracy. Therefore, even the white segregationists that hated him and rejected his politics understood the significance of what was being said. This explains to a considerable extent why most white Americans refuse to question the meaning of "whiteness," or acknowledge how white racial identity is a social construction built on the trans-Atlantic slave trade, chattel slavery, and massive American Indian removal to reservations. White Americans have been taught to handle the common history they share with African Americans very differently than black Americans. Most cannot comprehend that virtually every major advance in this nation's democratic institutions was directly caused, or profoundly influenced by the black American struggle for freedom.

Conversely, it would have been impossible for African Americans not to have been influenced by America's master narrative and thereby led to deny the validity of our own material culture and experiences. The desire for inclusion and the benefits of selectively forgetting America's "mistakes" are powerful incentives toward assimilation. After all, we have coexisted side by side in the same geographical space for hundreds of years, sharing in many respects a common language of memory.

Yet much of the historical evidence drawn directly from black people themselves indicates that, even during the time of slavery, although white and black Americans may have spoken a common language, they interpreted daily events in strikingly divergent ways. As the editors of *Remembering Slavery: African Americans Talk About Their Personal Experiences of Slavery and Freedom* make clear, white Southerners uniformly "emphasized the close personal relationships between slaves and owners while downplaying the violence and exploitation on which slavery rested. They glorified the docile 'darkies' who had served so faithfully, the loyal mammies who had nursed both white and black children, and the trusted servants who protected the plantation against the hated Yankees." Formerly enslaved African Americans and their children, conversely, "described the endless indignities of chattel bondage; its numerous perils to family life; the trauma that accompanied beatings, mutilations, and murders; the prohibitions against education and religious worship; the denial of the basic civil rights they would claim as their own during Reconstruction."

At the beginning of the twentieth century, some African-American intellectuals recognized that the generation that had personally experienced enslavement was rapidly disappearing, and that some measures to preserve and document their personal stories had to be initiated. In the 1920s, black scholars at racially segregated institutions such as Fisk University, Kentucky State University, and Southern University in Louisiana began to interview and document the lives of former slaves. During the Great Depression, through the initiative of Lawrence Reddick at Kentucky State University, John and Ruby Lomax, Zora Neal Hurston, and many others, thousands of ex-slave narratives were recorded and collected as part of the Federal Writers' Project. Despite fierce criticisms by most white historians at the time—on the grounds that formerly enslaved blacks' testimonials constituted tainted and biased information, lacking the objectivity of white public documents or white observers—these early oral historians understood that the historical knowledge produced by the slaves themselves had to be preserved in order for it to be conveyed to successive generations.

It is perhaps not a coincidence that during the current conservative political period—with the dismantling of affirmative action, the elimination of minority economic set asides and scholarship programs, and other reforms—African-American efforts have turned towards preserving the lessons and personal examples from a more heroic era.

Histories of slavery and its aftermath based on the memories of enslaved African Americans are undoubtedly more accurate at documenting the true indignity of slavery than the writings and reflections of their former owners, but even they must be viewed critically. A paper by the Popular Memory Group, a collective of historians at the University of Birmingham's Center for Contemporary Cultural Studies working in the late 1970s and early 1980s, observes that private memories of individuals cannot "be readily unscrambled from the effects of dominant historical discourses. It is often these that supply the very terms by which a private history is thought through. Memories of the past are, like all common-sense forms, strangely composite constructions, resembling a kind of geology, the selective sedimentation of past traces."

A broad review of the thousands of ex-slave oral histories compiled by the Federal Writers' Project in the 1930s reveals, in the words of Robin D. G. Kelley, "the complicated character of their recollections." Many former slaves giving their oral histories spoke "in vague generalities that owed at least as much to their suspicions about the questioners as to the dimness of their recollections." Others tried to "cloak their experiences" by describing as benign their own history as a slave, while recounting the brutalities and violence of daily life for slaves at nearby plantations. Former slaves generally preferred to focus on the "immediate past," especially their role "in the drama of emancipation," rather than providing a detailed recounting of their grandparents' or parents' experiences from stories they themselves had learned as children.

The most well-publicized effort to preserve the living legacy of the recent African-American past is the History Makers project, launched in 1999 by attorney and television producer Julieanna L. Richardson. The goal of History Makers is to produce an archive of five thousand first person narratives of African Americans "both well known and unsung." Richardson's objective, the project's literature states, "is to show the world that African American history is American history and that African American History

Makers number not in the hundreds, but in the thousands."
Toward that end, History Makers has hosted a variety of
multimedia productions and events, including "An Evening
with Harry Belafonte," televised on the Public Broadcasting
System network, and "An Evening with Ossie Davis and
Ruby Dee" at Chicago's Art Institute, and "Pioneers in the
Struggle," a television documentary and educational CD-
ROM tracing the history of blacks who have served in the
Illinois State Assembly since 1877.

To finance this extraordinary effort, Richardson raised
$2.4 million through grants and private donations and from
foundations. A similar multimedia effort, led by former
ABC News correspondent Renee Poussaint and philanthro-
pist Camille Cosby, is the National Visionary Leadership
Project. This project identifies African Americans over the
age of seventy who have made significant contributions to
the social, cultural, economic, and political life of both
black America and the country as a whole. Richardson describes her project and other efforts as "preserving living
history."

While these and other documentary efforts are indeed
admirable and worthy of generous support, they separate
history from theory and politics in certain respects. Richardson seeks to place the historical narrative of blacks in
America into America's mainstream narrative about itself.
What must be accomplished instead is the subversion of
the master narrative itself. This must involve to a great extent the deconstruction of the legitimacy of white identity,
and must uncover the massive evidence of crimes against

humanity routinely sanctioned by corporate and state power. The corpses must be exhumed, not for purposes of ritualistic ancestor worship, but to study the forensic evidence to determine who was actually responsible for the crimes that have been committed. C. L. R. James, in *The Black Jacobins,* astutely observed that "revenge has no place in politics." Yet a culture without a deep reservoir drawing upon collective memory inevitably ceases to exist. Our purpose should not be to indict those who were responsible for these crimes, but to make the descendants of both victims and criminals see themselves and their own histories in new ways.

Columbia University's Center for Contemporary Black History, which I initiated in 2002, has started several "living black history" projects, based on a theoretical approach that embraces the political nature of history. The objective of these research projects was not just to educate and inform, but to transform the objective material, cultural conditions, and subordinate status of marginalized groups through informed civic engagement. We must reconstruct America's memory about itself, and our collective past, in order to reimagine its future.

One of the first "living history" projects our center developed, Freedom Summer 2004, was in partnership with Myrlie Evers-Williams, former national chairman of the National Association for the Advancement of Colored People (NAACP). We proposed the mobilization of about 250 college-aged students across the state of Mississippi to organize "freedom schools" and register thousands of voters. The project, developed in mid-2003, was planned to coincide with the fortieth anniversary of the historic "Freedom Summer" of 1964, when one thousand Northern, mostly white students traveled to Mississippi to organize voters in poor, black, rural communities. That summer in Mississippi, one thousand civil rights organizers were arrested and eighty seriously beaten, thirty-nine black churches and thirty black schools were firebombed, and five civil rights activists were killed.

Understandably, most white Mississippians still desperately want the world to forget this terrible history. However, our objective was also to bring attention to the living history of everyday, average white Southerners, especially those few courageous souls who had opposed Jim Crow segregation. As historian James Green has noted, "the monumental history of the South has been dominated by the elites and dedicated to the memories of generals and politicians." A survey of National Park Service landmarks in the South found that virtually none highlight poor whites, those "forgotten men and women who toiled in the fields and the factories, the mines and the mills that produced the region's wealth."

A project like the proposed Freedom Summer 2004 is important not just for its value as a commemoration of the past, but because it is something so direly needed to help ensure a better future. In 1965 Congress passed the Voting Rights Act, and the percentage of registered black voters soared from 6.7 percent in 1964 to over 61 percent in 1967. The Jim Crow laws were overturned. Nonetheless, second class citizenship has reemerged across the South, because of the adoption of repressive voter laws. In Mississippi, a citizen convicted of a felony loses the right to vote for life. Thirty percent of black male adults in Mississippi today cannot vote. The projected goal of the Freedom Summer 2004 field organizing campaign was to focus greater public awareness on the unfairness of these restrictions.

Coordinating our efforts with several members of the Mississippi Legislative Black Caucus, our plan was to push for the adoption of liberalized voter laws. Part of that new voter rights campaign would include a series of public educational forums and civic conversations, where white and black Mississippians would be encouraged to talk candidly and honestly about the state's turbulent racial history. We planned to incorporate old and new films, newspaper accounts, photos, and recent interviews with the veterans of the original Freedom Summer into multimedia materials generated during the summer's activities. We also proposed the creation of a "Families of the Disfranchised" group, documenting how losing the right to vote negatively affects everyday people, white and black. A multimedia case study of the historical struggle for voting rights in Mississippi could bridge the past and present, helping to create a more democratic future.

The grant proposal for this project was circulated to a number of major foundations throughout 2003 and early 2004, without success. Some funders reviewed the project and dismissed it as being "a walk down the Civil Rights Movement Memory Lane," nothing more than a symbolic gesture to a past that had little relationship with the state's current problems. One program officer, representing a foundation with a history of supporting criminal justice-related projects, suggested that I ask my friend Russell Simmons (Def Jam cofounder and hip-hop millionaire) to "bankroll this enterprise." "We all love Myrlie," this program officer sympathized, but this entire effort was simply "too political."

Several years before the formal establishment of the Center, I had become aware of the tremendous potential for utilizing the tools of multimedia digital technology in reinterpreting the past. In 2000, I participated with several Columbia faculty in the construction of a Web-based multimedia version of W. E. B. Du Bois's classic *The Souls of Black Folk* that was designed for classroom use. *The Souls of Black Folk* multimedia study environment embedded into the text several hundred photographs, audio recordings of Du Bois, film clips, and historical documents, which made the book literally come alive, especially for a generation of students who had grown up watching MTV and navigating the Internet.

The success of the *Souls* multimedia study environment inspired the production of even more ambitious multimedia educational resources. Working with our technology partner, the Columbia Center for New Media Teaching and Learning, my research assistants and I created in 2001 an electronic seminar, or e-course, "Malcolm X: Life After Death." From 2001 to 2004, with the financial support of Columbia's provost, we constructed an elaborately rich multimedia version of *The Autobiography of Malcolm X.* This ambitious effort required a staff of more than twenty annotation writers, editors, researchers, and web technicians. The final product presented the entire text online, with hundreds of hyperlinks throughout the text linked to critical annotations, audio, video, photographic images, and other resources. I interviewed a number of individuals who had worked closely with Malcolm X, some of whom provided eyewitness accounts of his 1965 assassination. We also located rare government documents pertaining to the U.S. government's surveillance of Malcolm X, both while he was inside the Nation of Islam and after his break from the organization. These materials, when combined with the oral history interviews conducted with Malcolm X's co-workers, shed new light on the actual activities of this still widely misunderstood African-American leader. Through these technologies and multidisciplinary methods of historical investigation, it became possible to create "new history"—a history that more accurately presents the authentic story of black people from their own point of view, as they lived it.

Another productive and illuminating approach to understanding past events is the critical reconstruction of the "past" with realistic "alternative pasts" that were possible. Historian Paul B. Miller has described this as "counterfactual history," a critical inquiry "grounded in facts" but creating possible "alternative pasts" or different historical trajectories. For instance, in Miller's research he pursued the question, what if the Allies had bombed and destroyed

Auschwitz and other Nazi concentration camps during World War II? In doing so, wouldn't the Allies have saved thousands, perhaps millions of Jewish lives? A combination of counterfactual inquiry and traditional methodology has led scholars to "hitherto silent sources. . . . When you ask a question about something that never took place, you have to analyze all possible reasons for its not taking place, including those given by the very people who had the power to make history turn out differently." In African-American history, there have been a number of decisive moments when the trajectory of black history could have progressed in any of several very different ways, leading to qualitatively different outcomes.

One example that immediately comes to mind is the issue of land redistribution and property ownership to exslaves following the American Civil War in 1865. Forty acres allocated to each African-American family in 1865 would have called for the seizure of only forty million acres of farmland by the federal government. Part of this could have been accomplished had Congress passed Thaddeus Stevens's proposal to confiscate the property of all former slaveholders who owned two hundred or more slaves. The lack of comprehensive land ownership and financial assets by blacks has been perhaps the most important element in the racialized inequity that exists up to the present. Imagining plausible alternative scenarios based on factual evidence can help us understand the consequences of history, while exposing the connections between history and power.

The failure to enact land reform during Reconstruction paved the way for the rise of sharecropping and debt peonage, which burdened millions of African Americans with poverty for generations. A similar dynamic of economic underdevelopment occurred in the mid- to late twentieth century with a disinvestment of billions of dollars from America's central cities, setting into motion new processes of racialization that resulted in today's prison industrial complex, and what Mike Davis terms "dead cities," which are of course predominantly black and brown. Banks and savings-and-loans "pumped capital out of the inner city but refused to loan it back, especially to Black-majority neighborhoods," Davis notes. "Instead they drained Northeastern savings to the Sunbelt, where they stoked a massive speculative building boom. Local banks in Brooklyn in the 1970s, for example, committed less than 6 per cent of mortgages to their home borough: fully 63 per cent of local savings were exported to Florida and elsewhere."

This massive economic underdevelopment triggered destructive social forces that had concrete racial consequences. One way to understand this is from the perspective of the physical environment over time. Nearly three decades ago, photographer Camilla Vergara embarked on a monumental project in which she photographed random buildings in some of America's most depressed inner-cities, such as Detroit, the Bronx, and Newark. Vergara's objective was to create a visual archive documenting the cycle of urban social death. Returning to the same photographic sites, month after month, year after year, a graphic portrait of social death became clear. For African Americans, it illustrates that while the signs reading "white" and "colored" may have been taken down, redlining policies of banks help manufacture the physical environments, reproducing racialized lives. Through the camera's lens, a hidden history of structural racism is revealed. This visual study helps us understand that history, while being the product of individual decisions and choices, takes place within larger institutional contexts and socioeconomic environments. As Karl Marx noted in "The Eighteenth Brumaire of Louis Bonaparte," "Men make their own history, but they do not make it just as they please, they do not make it by themselves, but under circumstances directly encountered, given and transmitted from the past."

Let us therefore approach the construction of a new black history from the vantage point of the evolution of black consciousness over time. The state of being critically self-aware prefigures both a sense of power and a capacity for action. For the oppressed in racially stratified societies, self-awareness involves a fundamental recognition that many common practices of daily life retard one's development. As racialized populations reflect upon the accumulated concrete experiences of their own lives, the lives of others who share their situation, and even those who have died long ago, a process of discovery unfolds that begins to restructure how they understand the world and their place within it. That journey of discovery can produce a desire to join with others to build initiatives that create space, permitting the renewal or survival of a group, or a celebration of its continued existence despite the forces arrayed against it.

Knowledgeable civic actors can draw important lessons from history, which does incrementally increase civic capacity. Historical amnesia blocks the construction of potentially successful social movements. As the gap between the past, present, and future diminishes, individuals can acquire a greater sense of becoming the "makers" of their own history. Thus, for the oppressed, the act of reconstructing history is inextricably linked to the political practices, or *praxis,* of transforming the present and future.

Mapping Black Political Culture

Leadership, Intellectuals, and Resistance

Intellectual leaders are not detached from their social milieus; typically they seek to change it. . . . Some intellectuals perhaps long after their time—pervasively influence the intellectual temper of an epoch and the thinking and actions of politicians. The concept of intellectual *leadership* brings in the role of *conscious purpose* drawn from values.
— JAMES MCGREGOR BURNS

A CENTRAL QUESTION IN THE CONSTRUCTION OF US social history is, what makes the African-American people so *different* from most other Americans in their political and social attitudes, behaviors, and civic practices? The collective experience of pain and hardship, suffering and sacrifice has given African Americans a unique perspective from which our consciousness has been forged. Undeniably, the edges of that racialized sensibility have frayed as advances have been made, but its core values remain,

reflecting the collective pride of group endurance and per-
severance. We know within ourselves, as Dr. Martin Luther
King Jr. reminded us a generation ago, that the moral arc of
the universe, while extremely long, does appear to bend toward justice. Or, in the words of Albert Einstein, we have
long believed that God does not play dice.

African-American political culture was hammered together over the years with the imperfect tools of survival
and capacity-building from below, evolving and oscillat-
ing constantly and often unpredictably between outright
accommodation and overt resistance. Violence has generally remained the option of last resort, while nonviolent
direct action protests, voting, and negotiations have historically proven more effective. An uneven mixture of tactical approaches, most grounded in measurable results,
came to dominate black political practices. Malcolm X's
famous "ballot or bullet" formulation, declared in Cleveland, Ohio, on April 3, 1964, only echoed the older, more
provocatively insurrectionist "Let your motto be resistance!" issued in Henry Highland Garnet's speech at the
1843 Negro Convention in Buffalo, New York, and both
are indelibly etched into African-American perceptions of
power and the definition of what constitutes successful
approaches toward achieving our collective goals.

Another, more interesting, way of examining this question is to ask, why are white Americans different in their
political behavior from most African Americans? From
the outset, European immigrants—who ultimately came
to think of themselves as whites—have shared a basic set
of experiences sharply at odds with those of black people.

The general pattern of the white population's development in North America was emigration, resettlement, ethnic consolidation, and ultimately assimilation.

Within that broad framework, of course, were significant differences between ethnic groups. As historian Ronald Takaki reminds us, "English immigrants and their descendants . . . possessed inordinate power to define American culture and make public policy" from the outset. Conversely, Asian immigrants were usually classified as "'heathen,' exotic, and inassimilable," the perpetual "'strangers' coming to a different shore." Likewise, a substantial Mexican population—here well before 1848—found itself "enclosed by America's expanding borders." A half century later Puerto Ricans, Hawaiians, and for a time Filipinos would suffer similar encounters. Nevertheless, it was the African American who dwelled at the "bottom" of what became America's racialized social body.

The black journey through the unfolding drama of American history has been characterized by enslavement or capture through physical coercion, involuntary transfer in cargo holds across the south Atlantic, immediate sale of those who survived the arduous voyage, generations of slavery, later generations under Jim Crow segregation, and urban ghettoization in the early to late twentieth century. This collective experience has been marked by brief periods of intense disruption and social instability, leading to mass migrations (involuntary and voluntary), followed by the fragile and difficult process of resettlement, and the reconstruction of kinship, networks, and cultural and social institutions. The sole constant throughout, until relatively recently, is the black

Americans' status as political and social pariah. The burden of race has been omnipresent and, for nearly everyone of African descent, inescapable. Not surprisingly, blacks have developed a profound ambivalence about the entire political experiment commonly called "The United States of America."

This may help to explain the bittersweet combination of boundless hope and enduring hostility which characterizes so much African-American civic discourse, past and present. In 1852 a small group of white abolitionists asked Frederick Douglass, a former slave, to speak at their Fourth of July celebration. The rich ironies of the scenario completely escaped them. To Douglass, however, the event was the perfect venue for venting his enormous anger and anguish about America:

> What to the American slave is your Fourth of July? I answer, a day that reveals to him more than all other days of the year, the gross injustice and cruelty to which he is the constant victim. To him your celebration is a sham; your boasted liberty an unholy license; your national greatness, swelling vanity; your sounds of rejoicing are empty and heartless; your denunciation of tyrants, brass-fronted impudence; your shouts of liberty and equality, hollow mockery; your prayers and hymns, your sermons and thanksgivings, with all your religious parade and solemnity, are to him mere bombast, fraud, deception, impiety, and hypocrisy—a thin veil to cover up crimes which would disgrace a nation of savages. There is not a nation of the entire

earth guilty of practices more shocking and bloody
than the people of these United States at this very hour.

Most likely perturbed, Douglass's white friends would
have listened to this ranting politely, possibly with puzzled
expressions, wondering what the fuss was all about. However, if any Jewish Americans were present in Rochester to
hear Frederick Douglass that day, theirs would have been
the few heads nodding knowingly in agreement. Despite the
physical face of their "whiteness," the lives of American
Jews were also defined by unfair exclusion, ethnic segregation, and discrimination. They desperately sought to maintain and honor the rich traditions and rituals that defined
their cultural identity, but pursued at the same time the ad-
vantages of assimilation and civic participation enjoyed by
the white mainstream. These were strategic alternatives and
options that, until quite recently, African Americans were
denied by the intimate black boundaries of, in George Lam-
ming's memorable image, the "castles of their skin."

Since European colonization of the North American continent, four overlapping "racial domains" have been constructed. Each racial domain represents a particular set of
dominant racist stereotypes as well as the pervasive institutional racism codified at the time. The first racial domain
constructed in the United States—the "peculiar institution"
of legal slavery—lasted nearly 250 years. Roughly 60 percent of the entire historical experience of African-American
people was framed by the inescapable reality of being legally
defined as noncitizens and private property.

Relegated beyond white society's boundaries, the Negro's status embodied everything that nonblack immigrants desperately sought to avoid and to transcend. As U.S. Supreme Court Justice Roger B. Tawney succinctly put the matter in the 1857 *Dred Scott v. Sanford* decision, Negroes had always "been regarded as beings of an inferior order and altogether unfit to associate with the white race, either in social or political relations, and so far inferior that they had no rights which the white man was bound to respect."

After a decade of racial reform during the Reconstruction period, a second racial domain descended with the weight of an iron curtain: Jim Crow segregation. Some of the chief characteristics of this racial domain were the physical exclusion of blacks from nearly every aspect of public and civic life, including voting, running for elective office, and access to public accommodations, quality public education, and many social services. Violence, in the brutal form of thousands of lynchings across the southern states, reinforced the white supremacist regime.

The increasing mechanization of southern agriculture, the growing availability of industrial jobs in the northeastern and midwestern states, and the intensification of racial atrocities against African-American communities in the South all contributed to the Great Migration of blacks, beginning in significant numbers by 1915. A third racial domain came into existence as millions of African Americans migrated north to central cities.

This third racial domain was characterized by the rise of ghettoization—the hypersegregation and confinement of blacks in impoverished urban districts. Harlem in northern

Manhattan, Brooklyn's Bedford-Stuyvesant, Cleveland's Hough, Chicago's South Side, and Watts in inner-city Los Angeles all became America's version of South Africa's notorious Bantustans. This process of racial exclusion was made possible, in part, because the Democratic Party's primary bastions of power were based on either the old urban political machines controlled by white ethnics or by the conservative white segregationist leaders dominating the South's Democratic Party apparatus. As late as 1964, there were only five black representatives in the House, none in the Senate, none on the Supreme Court, and only one hundred holding elective office anywhere in the country.

The Civil Rights Act of 1964 and the Voting Rights Act of 1965 ended the legal regime of Jim Crow segregation, but not its long-lasting effects within American political culture. The black freedom movement, in its civil rights and Black Power phases, demanded a fundamental restructuring of America's racial hierarchies, in both the South and in the nation's northern ghettoes. The political concessions that were granted, while preserving structural racism within economic life, substantially changed political and social relations between whites and blacks. The major reforms such as affirmative action, race-based college scholarships, and minority economic set-asides gave birth to a large and increasingly affluent African-American middle class.

In the 1970s and 1980s, many of the public administrative responsibilities for running the most de-industrialized, welfare-swollen central cities were handed over to black elected officials as well. They were confronted with ungovernable situations in cities with declining tax bases during the conservative fiscal austerity known as Reaganism. African-American elected officials as a group tended to respond to these challenges by distancing themselves from the heritage of community-based activism and grass-roots organizing that characterized much of the 1960s and 1970s. They sought to minimize their own identification with historical interests articulated by civil rights groups by appealing to their electoral constituencies on issues that were "race-neutral," stressing policy agendas that would restore confidence within the corporate community. Their efforts to halt deindustrialization and the flight of capital from decaying core cities were only partially successful, even in the best of circumstances.

It was on these foundations that a fourth racial domain came into existence in the late twentieth century. This new racial domain, the contemporary political economy of racialized domination, is just one facet of an emerging worldwide system of human exploitation, the rise of which has coincided with the emergence of transnational globalization. The fourth racial domain has two main interdependent aspects, economic and political. The mass unemployment of the minority labor force has relegated vast populations into the informal and "underground" economies. The growth of informal underground, and sometimes illegal, economies has coincided with an unprecedented reliance on the criminal justice system—specifically penal institutions—to process, warehouse, and dehumanize racial minorities who have become unnecessary as producers in the formal labor market. Consequently, the millions of citizens who have been convicted of felonies have been eliminated either temporarily or permanently from meaningful civic participation.

This trend of mass disfranchisement has created a qualitatively new ethnic dynamic within national political culture. Moreover, the growth of extreme class stratification and spatial segmentation among blacks has created ideologically conservative black constituencies, and these elites are increasingly allied with the corporate and political establishment. The leadership of black America was poorly prepared to confront this grave new world of color-blind structural racism—a racism without overtly public racists. The "white" and "colored" signs had long since disappeared, but too many black leaders still function as if they still exist. It was all much simpler then, standing defiantly at Selma's Edmund Pettus Bridge singing "We Shall Overcome" so long ago.

Over time—as one racial domain evolved into the next—two general strategies for racial advancement became clear. One approach, gathering favor among the most privileged of African Americans, was a fierce rejection of racialization, isolation, and exclusion in all of their guises and institutional forms. This strategy relied on alliances with sympathetic whites dedicated to racial reforms, and emphasized governmental actions preserving citizenship, civil liberties, and constitutionally grounded rights. The overriding goal was the merger of blacks' interests with those of the country. The boundaries of blackness, it was proposed, could one day permeate the national bodies of power.

During the periods of black enslavement, Civil War, and Reconstruction, this political approach led to the abolition of slavery, universal male suffrage, and the modification of the U.S. Constitution to ensure equality under the law as an inviolable right for all. Under the post–Jim Crow regime of de facto segregation, the advocates of this perspective consolidated behind the NAACP, the Congress of Racial Equality, and the National Urban League. Their most eloquent and effective spokespersons, including Frederick Douglass, William Monroe Trotter, Adam Clayton Powell Jr., and Dr. Martin Luther King Jr., spread these ideas among national and international audiences. By the 1950s this strategic perspective was commonly called "integration."

Integration was never universally accepted among African Americans as the best method or approach for achieving racial reform. Beginning early in the nineteenth century, many black educators, clergy, and civic leaders proposed that people of African descent in America possessed innate qualities of mind and culture worth preserving. For example, speaking before a black "church congress" held in Richmond, Virginia, in October 1882, noted scholar Alexander Crummell presented an address called "A Defense of the Negro Race," which provides an excellent expression of this alternative viewpoint. "The Negro race is a living, not a dead race—alive in the several respects of industry, acquisitiveness, education, and religious aspiration," Crummell declared. Having returned to the United States after a twenty-year exile in West Africa, Crummell had the conviction that there were "certain vital qualities inherent in the race." Traditional African leaders, Crummell advised, instinctively "trust those universal and unfailing tendencies of TRUTH, JUSTICE, and EQUITY, which have ever attended their history on this continent!"

Leaders like Crummell favored the construction of cultural, social, and spiritual institutions based on black heritage and group traditions. This race-based approach to political agitation eventually came to include the advocacy of black entrepreneurship and private ownership of real estate, and the construction of black-centered or "Afro centric" rituals, historical narratives, and cultural performance, fostering independence and agency among blacks. The creation of black political organizations offered informal alternatives to the representative bodies of the U.S. government. This strategy for racial advancement became known as "black nationalism" even before the emergence of Marcus Garvey's Universal Negro Improvement Association in 1914.

These two ideological positions—integration and black nationalism—were never mutually exclusive; indeed, adherence to one set of views about race and power or another was for most African Americans situational and open to debate. In many respects, these two ideological strands are complimentary, yet competing, parts of a splintered whole. Both ideological tendencies, for example, actively supported the construction of rituals and cultural events that celebrated the democratic aspirations and national identity of African Americans. White Americans sang "The Star

Spangled Banner," while African Americans of all ideological hues took pride in their own national anthem, "Lift Ev'ry Voice and Sing."

Because African Americans were effectively excluded from participating in America's democratic institutions even after their emancipation from bondage, it is hardly surprising that they devised their own rituals and civic events to celebrate the meaning of freedom. On June 19, 1865, when Major General Gordon Granger and federal troops landed in Galveston, Texas, and declared the state's 250,000 slaves freed, African Americans throughout Texas celebrated the date henceforth as "Juneteenth." It didn't matter that the Emancipation Proclamation had been signed by Abraham Lincoln in 1862, and had taken effect on January 1, 1863. To paraphrase Mao, freedom for the oppressed frequently is achieved from the barrel of a gun. As black Texans migrated into the Midwest and northeastern states, and subsequently to the Pacific, their Juneteenth celebration became part of national African-American culture. In 1980, Texas acknowledged the political clout of the state's African-American electorate by making Juneteenth an official, paid state holiday. In 2003, the District of Columbia recognized Juneteenth as an official holiday. In 2004, New York Republican governor George Pataki signed a bill establishing "Juneteenth Freedom Day" in New York state. By 2005, Juneteenth, usually observed on the third Saturday of June, had been recognized in seventeen states. The U.S. Congress recognized Juneteenth in a resolution passed in 1997.

Due to the omnipresence of white supremacy, African Americans were forced to construct their own civil society and democratic rituals, such as Juneteenth, that were a product of their collective struggles inside the territorial confines of the United States. By way of contrast, Cinco de Mayo, the major Mexican-American holiday, celebrates a military victory that occurred in 1862 in Mexico, not within the United States. Unlike Mexican Americans or Asian immigrants, Negroes were never, to employ Takaki's phrase, "strangers from a different shore." We had been here *before* white people actually thought of themselves *as white people*. Without relying too heavily on G. W. F. Hegel's dialectics, a bipolar racial template links black to white and white to black; both are necessary in order for "whiteness" to have any meaning.

To most white racists, the Negro was absolutely necessary (whereas the Jew, Filipino, Puerto Rican, Japanese, and Chinese were not), and this confronted African Americans with the inescapable reality of their terrible situation. The demand for cheap black labor had been a necessary component in the economic expansion of capitalism across North America. White capital would never "voluntarily" surrender its exploitation of black labor power, or the excessive profits generated by selling substandard consumer items and services to Negroes. Blacks fully recognized their oppression, but could not extricate themselves because their citizenship and national identity was tied to the United States. African-American national consciousness and identity is principally a product of America, not Africa. In effect, black

Americans are members of the national household, but are excluded from sitting at the dining room table with other family members. The classical expression of the dilemma blacks faced was best phrased by W. E. B. Du Bois:

> After the Egyptian and Indian, the Greek and Roman, the Teuton and Mongolian, the Negro is a sort of seventh son, born with a veil, and gifted with second-sight in this American world,—a world which yields him no true self-consciousness, but only lets him see himself through the revelation of the other world. It is a peculiar sensation, this double-consciousness, this sense of always looking at one's self through the eyes of others, of measuring one's soul by the tape of a world that looks on in amused contempt and pity. One ever feels his two-ness—an American, a Negro; two souls, two thoughts, two unreconciled strivings; two warring ideals in one dark body, whose dogged strength alone keeps it from being torn asunder. The history of the American Negro is the history of this strife,—this longing to attain self-conscious manhood, to merge his double self into a better and truer self. In this merging he wishes neither of the older selves to be lost.

Du Bois captured the essential American dilemma from the Negro's point of view: How could blacks enter fully into American democracy without becoming so completely and uncritically "American" that they ceased to exist as a unified and unique cultural group? Voluntary separation from whites created space for the successful construction of black institutions, but simultaneously distanced the African-American community from access to the technology, resources, and capital from which most whites benefited. However, submerging our nationalistic strivings meant cutting off precious psychological, cultural, political, and even kinship links to the black world. Finding the balance to achieve this unity of opposites was difficult for Du Bois and for subsequent generations of black intellectuals who would follow him. Richard Wright, James Baldwin, Harold Cruse, Amiri Baraka, and many others struggled with this dilemma, never quite finding the right balance. What all of these black intellectuals had in common, however, was that as political "actors" they operated in a relatively fixed racial universe, with whiteness at the center of that realm.

A history of the turbulent evolution and major shifts, successes, and setbacks within black consciousness between 1919 and 1945 illustrates that certain significant events—like the Great Depression, the outbreak of anticolonial agitation and mass nonviolent protests in India, the rise of communism and global warfare in the forties—created contexts for the development of individual leaders and intellectuals with certain distinctive qualities. Malcolm X, for example, was a product of all these events and social forces, and can be viewed as one representative of a transnational generation attempting to initiate black radical and revolutionary projects. Within his cohort, among those who struggled against colonialism and legal segregation were novelist/social critic James Baldwin, Julius Nyerere of Tanzania, Eduardo Mondlane of Mozambique, Agostinho Neto of Angola, Amilcar Cabral of Portuguese Guiné, Harold Cruse, Ella Baker, Vincent Harding, Septima Clark, Bayard Rustin, and of course, Dr. Martin Luther King Jr.

Malcolm X's closest counterpart in the post–World War II black diaspora was Frantz Fanon (1925–1961). Born in Martinique, Fanon became the leading theorist of the anti-colonial revolution against French rule in Algeria and author of *The Wretched of the Earth*. Like Malcolm X, Fanon was a relentless critic of "whiteness" and rejected the philosophy of nonviolence. Fanon believed that the oppressed had the right to use violence to defend themselves against the colonizer, and he felt that such violence was essential in purging the self-hatred and cultural dependency which characterized the minds of nonwhites within racist societies. An independent black consciousness was necessary if blacks were to remake both their world and themselves.

Fanon's *The Wretched of the Earth* illustrates how the psychological makeup of the colonized black mind leads to self-mutilation and the assimilation of white standards of beauty. Similarly, in *The Autobiography of Malcolm X*, Malcolm reflects back to his first experience of straightening or "conking" his hair; he admits "how ridiculous I was . . . stupid enough to stand there simply lost in admiration of my hair looking 'white.'" Fanon sharply condemns this desire to achieve "whiteness at any price." The black colonized mind desired "all manner of possession: to sit at the settler's table, to sleep in the settler's bed, with his wife if possible." Both Malcolm and Fanon attempted to instill a new racial identity among black people that rejected the materialistic values and cultural traditions of the white world. Fanon believed that blacks "must leave our dreams and abandon our old dreams. . . . Let us waste no time in sterile litanies and nauseating mimicry . . . if we want humanity to advance a step further, if we want to bring it up to a different level than that which Europe or America has shown it, then we must invent and we must make discoveries. . . . We must turn over a new leaf, we must work out new concepts, and try to set afoot a new man."

Both Malcolm X and Fanon also vigorously condemned the black bourgeoisie, the "house Negroes" who loyally supported the white power structure at the expense of the interests of the black masses. In his famous "Message to the Grassroots" address delivered in Detroit on November 10, 1963, Malcolm charged that black middle-class leaders committed to racial integration were ideologically descended from the plantation "Uncle Toms" of a century before:

> The slavemaster took Tom and dressed him well and even gave him a little education a *little* education; gave him a long coat and a top hat and made all the other slaves look up to him. Then he used Tom to control them. The same strategy that was used in those days is used today, by the same white man. He takes a Negro, a so-called Negro, and makes him prominent, builds him up, publicizes him, makes him a celebrity. And then he becomes a spokesman for Negroes—and a Negro leader.

The device Malcolm employed—the rewriting of slavery's history to emphasize class contradictions—forced open questions of divided political loyalties that frustrated the progress of the black freedom movement. In similar fashion, Fanon criticized the black middle class in colonial societies. Both men were presenting alternative histories of enslavement and colonialism from the vantage point of society's marginalized groups. In these ways, both were fostering a more revolutionary black consciousness that required the fundamental restructuring of their respective societies' institutional arrangements. Both Fanon and Malcolm knew that history's power could be employed to challenge white supremacy.

In the mass democratic struggles against American structural racism over the past 150 years—whether inspired by integrationist or black nationalist political projects and strategies—the issue of leadership has been critical. Black leaders from abolitionist Frederick Douglass to former presidential candidate Jesse Jackson have interpreted black leadership primarily as capacity-building from below: building structures of group advocacy and resistance that are genuinely and organically linked throughout black civil society and its varied institutions. Intellectuals who assumed leadership roles in the black community have in very general terms endeavored to make vital contributions to that struggle through their own work and research.

The cultivation of a leadership class requires the development of what can be termed "organic intellectuals": women and men who comprehend the challenges that confront their people, and who devise practical approaches that change their collective situation. As Antonio Gramsci so eloquently put it, "All men are intellectuals . . . [every man] is a 'philosopher,' an artist, a man of taste, he participates in a particular conception of the world, has a conscious line of moral conduct, and therefore contributes to sustain a conception of the world or to modify it, that is, to bring into being new modes of thought." In other words, the intellectual is not removed from the society, but instead conceives the spectrum of possibilities for a new social world, and through articulation seeks to persuade others to embrace that vision. "The new intellectual," Gramsci observed, "can no longer consist in eloquence, which is an exterior and momentary mover of feelings and passions, but in active participation in practical life, as constructor, organiser, 'permanent persuader' and not just a simple orator." This captures the essence of what Malcolm X attempted to accomplish, for himself and his people: to break the devastating mental shackles of dependency and self-hatred imposed by centuries of slavery and segregation, to imagine a world without white supremacy and black inferiority, and to construct strong social institutions to perpetuate and protect the cultures and communities created by people of African descent. Central to this effort is the contestation of the "master narrative" and the construction of an alternative history.

The African-American intellectual tradition, since the middle of the nineteenth century, has largely been anchored by three principles and practices. First, it has been "descriptive," that is, presenting the reality of black life and experience from the point of view of black people themselves.

Second, it has been "corrective," a concerted attempt to challenge and to critique the racism and stereotypes that have been ever present in the main discourse of white academic institutions. And third, this tradition has been "prescriptive," an intellectual orientation which consistently connected scholarship with collective struggle, social analysis with social transformation.

How should today's black intellectuals be judged within the historical development of black protest consciousness? It is a curious paradox that as the walls of legal racial segregation tumbled and the doors of opportunity were opened (briefly), producing the modern professional-managerial black elite, the overall character of African-American scholarship has become less politically committed to addressing the challenges of social injustice. African-American studies as an interdisciplinary field of scholarship is increasingly disengaged with the pressing problems of the urban poor. Today's elitist discourse of liberal multiculturalism speaks the safe language of symbolic representation, but rarely of resistance. Our scholarship indeed must be rigorous and objective, but if it lacks vision or is not informed in its substructure by passionate collective memory, how meaningful can it be to the one million African Americans who currently are incarcerated in this nation's correctional facilities?

Furthermore, today's young African Americans—one generation removed from the triumphs of the civil rights era—are increasingly disconnected and uninformed about their own heritage. Tragically, with the disappearance of legal segregation, the space that permitted the existence of numerous black institutions of civic society—fraternal organizations, historically black colleges, neighborhood associations, faith-based institutions, and many others—began to contract and collapse. These race-based structures embodied a sense of shared sacrifice and collective struggle, and imposed on their participants notions of obligation and responsibility to other African Americans. In this way, the collective lessons of the black historical experience were disseminated and preserved through informal processes of socialization. With the coming of integration, all of that changed. Millions of middle-class African Americans relocated to suburbia, and the vast majority of black college students by 1970 became enrolled in predominantly white universities and colleges. The informal networks for transmitting collective history began to break down.

The hip-hop generation that came of age during the 1990s has generally learned history from cable television, the Internet, and music videos, and tends to have, at best, a fragmentary comprehension of their own heritage of black resistance. True, the most progressive elements of hip-hop culture, represented by artists such as Dead Prez, Paris, Public Enemy, and Tupac Shakur, articulated a language of protest. Yet their creative talents rarely yielded new modes of collective intervention that could forcefully challenge the existing structures of political power and corporate capitalism.

Most African-American intellectuals, moreover, were slow to recognize that the old "race rules" that had rigidly defined black-white relations for hundreds of years were giving way to a new social reality that was neither democratic nor egalitarian. "Integration" and "black nationalism" had been fixed paradigms for racial engagement and group contestation, each employing their own tactical approaches to maximizing black access and resources. By the late twentieth century, these strategic approaches had been made anachronistic and irrelevant by the forces of history. What the black intelligentsia was reluctant to confront was the construction of a new social theory that could challenge the newest manifestations of structural racism in the age of globalization.

In this effort, black intellectuals must consciously draw upon their knowledge of the past, but not be imprisoned by it. The innumerable feuds, conflicts, and public confrontations that have characterized black political culture for several centuries (e.g., Delany versus Douglass, Washington versus Du Bois, Garvey versus Du Bois, Malcolm X versus King) have been widely examined. Much of the historical and sociological literature about these intense debates, it appears to me, misses the ideological forest for the personality trees.

The idea of fundamentally transforming state power was so remote that few considered this a serious or realistic option. Black Americans were never more than approximately 20 percent of the total settler population in mid-eighteenth-century British North America, and were only 10 to 12 percent of all U.S. citizens throughout the twentieth century. Racial strategies for group empowerment and representation had to be fashioned keeping in mind the day-to-day conditions of "race" in America. America's "race rules" seemed to most as powerful as the law of gravity. Yet globalization and the rapid, unprecedented emergence of global apartheid have overturned that traditional gravity and the old laws of racial motion. This requires a virtual revolution in their thinking: how they conceive of "politics," and what can be meaningfully accomplished within their collective interventions, both within the U.S. government and on the international stage. They must step outside of their preconceived notions of group advocacy to reimagine another model of politics.

A productive way to think about the challenge that now confronts black political culture may be drawn from the field of physics. For several centuries, Newtonian physics defined what was measured and known about the physical universe. Galileo had previously paved the way by establishing that different bodies all accelerate at equal speed in the same environment. Descartes, building on Galileo's insights, then suggested that physical laws of motion measured on earth could also be applied to the larger physical universe. These insights were grounded in their empirical observations; their mechanics made sense because they could be validated independently by others. From these and other scientific discoveries, Isaac Newton created what Einstein would later describe as a "privileged system" of laws, fixed in an absolutist frame, regarding all bodies at rest and in motion within finite space. Newton's achievement led, of course, to a scientific and philosophical revolution in humanity's understanding of the universe and our place within it.

It required nearly three centuries of scientific investigation to produce an Einstein, who in 1905 advanced the heretical thesis that these rules had to be scrapped. Newton's absolute laws only operated within a privileged framework, and had the effect of discounting or eliminating evidence that existed outside its own fixed paradigm. As Silvio Bergia writes, Einstein "based his construction on the principle of relativity, extended to all physical phenomena and expressed as the equivalence of all frames of reference 'for which the equations of mechanics held good,' i.e., inertial systems." Einstein further suggested "another postulate, 'which is only apparently irreconcilable within the former; namely, that light is always propagated in empty space with a definite velocity c which is independent of the state of motion of the emitting body.'" In plain English, Einstein had created a new scientific framework of relativity that could still accommodate all previous scientific facts that had seemed completely fixed.

What was perhaps Einstein's most cogent explanation of his theoretical revolution, for the nonscientific community, was presented in a 1933 lecture, "On the Method of Theoretical Physics." Einstein observed that "pure logical thinking cannot yield us any knowledge of the empirical world; all knowledge of reality starts from experience and ends in it. Propositions arrived at by purely logical means are completely empty as regards reality." Einstein's intuitive insight informed his radical rupture from scientific orthodoxy, which he defined as "fictitious" in character, in the sense of it being "'free' inventions of the human intellect, which cannot be justified either by the nature of that intellect or in any other fashion *a priori*." The fundamentals of Newtonian physics had been grounded in absolute laws about physical reality that appeared to be practical and consistent with all observable phenomena. But such absolutist laws also restricted logical inquiry into what Einstein defined as "independent conceptual elements" that could be "deduced from experience by 'abstraction'—that is to say, by logical means." Einstein's general theory of relativity, published in 1916, forced the entire scientific community to acknowledge that Newton's approach was erroneous, and that "one could take into account a significantly wider 'range of empirical facts,' and that, too, in a more satisfactory and complete manner, on a foundation quite different from the Newtonian."

Any conceptual break from the rigid orthodoxies of global apartheid and U.S. structural racism, then, forces upon us the necessity to delegitimize all existing privileged systems of racial hierarchies and categories, and simultaneously to construct a new social paradigm, even while taking into account all empirical and historical evidence about the transnational processes of racialization. From that new vantage point, black history can be seen as an evolving process through which its principal actors (black people) attained a critical knowledge or consciousness through time, in various geographical and political contexts.

The broad contours of the "spiritual strivings" toward collective black emancipation were defined by struggles to outlaw first chattel slavery, then legal racial segregation and colonialism, and finally to attain independence and integration into local states and global institutions as full citizens. The prime objective of these projects, I believe, was the achievement of a singular civic virtue, which I call "justice." In the United States, then, what has been widely interpreted as a bitter contestation between black nationalist and integrationist strategic approaches is not a fundamental conflict at all. Integrationists favored state-based reforms primarily through federal legislation and legal protection, because practical historical experience had taught African Americans that the *state,* and *only the state,* was their best protector. But "integration" in and of itself was not ultimately an objective goal. Similarly, the black nationalist project, carried to its logical conclusions today, could not separate itself from the global apartheid system, and the new racial domain's rapidly mutating racialized hierarchies. Only a new world order based on a democratic, civic foundation of justice could provide the necessary social universe that could truly emancipate black people. Malcolm X, among others, clearly understood this at the end of his life. We must simultaneously preserve the best traditions people of African descent have contributed to the world's civilization, while transforming the privileged system of white society itself—deconstructing "whiteness" and enriching democratic institutions through civic participation at all levels.

For these reasons, historical knowledge, drawn from the reservoir of past collective experience, is absolutely vital to the task of imagining new racial futures for African Americans and for all Americans. We cannot negotiate a new, more democratic society until we understand what we have actually experienced as a nation and as a people. We cannot overcome the racist stereotypes and continued stigmatization of blacks that still persist to this day until we have a fuller appreciation of how women and men of remarkable courage devised methods of collective resistance, fighting for the democratic rights that enhanced the quality of life for all citizens. By documenting and preserving the past, and by promoting civic conversations about the historical struggles to dismantle institutionalized injustice, we build new possibilities for public dialogue about the real challenges that all Americans face in this brave new world of ours.

Resurrecting the Radical Du Bois

It is clear today that the salvation of American Negroes lies in socialism. They should support all measures and men who favor the welfare state: they should vote for government ownership of capital in industry; they should favor strict regulation of corporations and their public ownership; they should vote to prevent monopoly from controlling the press and the publishing of opinions. They should favor public ownership and control of water, electric, and atomic power; they should stand for a clean ballot, the encouragement of third parties, independent candidates, and the elimination of graft and gambling on television and even in churches.

—W. E. B. Du Bois

[W. E. B. Du Bois was] a true son of the intellectuals who founded the United States in 1776. Devoted as he was to righting the injustices of coloured people, he came in time to see his famous aphorism, that the problem of the twentieth century was the problem of the colour line, in a wider context.

—C. L. R. James

IT WAS UNQUESTIONABLY THE SOCIAL EVENT OF THE year. On the evening of April 27, 2003, more than eight thousand people paid a minimum of $150 each to attend the Detroit chapter of the NAACP's Fight for Freedom Fund Dinner. Thousands of well-groomed black men struck poses in tuxedos and dark business suits while thousands of African-American women gracefully glided across the arena floor splendidly attired in evening gowns and sparkling jewelry. The purpose of the night's historic celebration was to mark the one hundredth anniversary of the publication of *The Souls of Black Folk,* by William Edward Burghardt Du Bois. The vast Cobo Hall, Detroit's largest indoor arena, was literally overflowing with the elite group once described by W. E. B. Du Bois as the "Talented Tenth"—the most affluent, best-educated sector of black America. Among those seated at the main dais—the Cobo Arena was so cavernous that there were actually four daises—were Michigan's governor, one senator, several congressmen, the chief executive officer of Daimler-Chrysler Corporation, and Russell Simmons, the nation's leading hip-hop mogul. The gala's organizers placed a complimentary copy of *The Souls of Black Folk* at each individual place setting.

As the evening's keynote speaker I had been assigned the task of explaining, over the clatter of silverware and the steady background beat of Motown, the central ideas advanced by Du Bois in his classic work. My job was to link the book's significance to the particular challenges confronting black Americans in the twenty-first century. Yet it was a personal challenge to keep my mind on my lecture before the thousands of celebrants who had come to gossip, drink, joke, and parade proudly before the innumerable cameras.

Sitting immediately to my left was Russell Simmons, his demeanor as casual as his dress. An endless stream of eager young people clustered below our banquet table with CDs of their music, hoping to give them to Simmons. He graciously thanked all of the aspiring artists, advising them to hand over their demos to his Def Jam assistant seated nearby. After the entrees were served, as the stream of undiscovered musicians continued unabated, I asked Russell how he managed to keep things in perspective. Simmons explained with a smile that the secret lay in understanding that "life is like being in a movie—just enjoy scenes as they unfold." I appreciated his philosophical detachment, but the sociologist in me could not help but feel somewhat disconcerted by the surreal scene that was taking place all around us.

Sitting to my right was the chairman of the Daimler-Chrysler Corporation, and next to him was the governor of Michigan. Both were impeccably dressed and relentlessly gracious. I couldn't help but wonder, did they have a clue who W. E. B. Du Bois really was? How would they have treated him if they had been around in his day? Have they actually read the book that we're allegedly all honoring on this night? Or was their jovial appearance on the stage merely an acknowledgment of the substantial economic and political clout that had been accumulated by Detroit's African-American professional, entrepreneurial, and managerial class? Regardless of their motives, the representatives of corporate America and the transnational conglomerates were prominently present and proudly financing what the Detroit press announced was the "largest sit-down banquet" in the country.

Prior to the event the local media promoted Du Bois as being among the pantheon of America's greatest thinkers and the prime political architect of the Civil Rights Movement. Few in the audience probably knew that in 1951 the U.S. Justice Department had arrested and tried Du Bois unsuccessfully, accusing him of being an unlicensed representative of a foreign power, namely the Soviet Union. During the "Great Fear" of McCarthyism, *The Souls of Black Folk* and other works by Du Bois were frequently removed from libraries as examples of communist-inspired propaganda. Black America's poet laureate, Langston Hughes—after giving humiliating witness before Senator Joseph McCarthy's subcommittee—removed Du Bois from a revised edition of *Famous American Negroes.* The NAACP conspicuously chose not to sponsor the public celebration of Du Bois' ninetieth birthday in 1958, an event that attracted an audience of over a thousand to New York's Roosevelt Hotel. The hostility and fear once attached to Du Bois's name was still so strong right up until the moment of his death on August 27, 1963, that he remained highly problematic to the mainstream leadership of the Civil Rights Movement. Indeed, at the historic August 28, 1963, March on Washington, NAACP leader Roy Wilkins announced Du Bois's recent demise to the mass demonstration, emphasizing "the fact that in his later years Dr. Du Bois chose another path."

Wilkins's words of admonition were either forgotten or ignored forty years later by a new generation of NAACP leaders at *The Souls of Black Folk* centennial celebration. Still, if Du Bois's legacy had been accepted by the NAACP, it was clear on this night that his radical intellect had not been fully embraced. The gala event occurred at the same time that U.S. troops launched a military invasion of Iraq, a Third World conflict Du Bois certainly would have opposed. The Bush Administration was aggressively seeking to quell domestic protest and civil dissent by implementing measures of the Patriot Act—provisions that might have defined an activist like Du Bois as subversive. Aside from my own remarks, however, little of this was part of the orchestrated agenda for the evening. Other speakers, in a mantra of repetition, framed their acknowledgments of Du Bois's greatness around several memorable phrases, both drawn from *Souls*: that the "Negro is a sort of seventh son, born with a veil" and gifted with a "double consciousness" or a kind of "two-ness—an American, a Negro; two souls, two thoughts, two unreconciled strivings," and that the "problem of the twentieth century is the problem of the color line."

The official literature produced for the occasion offered little in the way of interpretation concerning the lasting significance of *Souls* and its relationship to contemporary African-American issues. In the banquet brochure, "*The Souls of Black Folk*: 100 Years Later," Detroit Mayor Kwame Kilpatrick suggested that the dinner's theme was truly relevant in 2003, as "African-Americans continue to face many of the same challenges our community faced a

century ago." The lessons of *Souls* and the continuing work
of the NAACP were dedicated to encouraging "all people of
color to work together to level the playing field and ensure
equal opportunity for everyone." Even more complex and
equally problematic was the statement of congratulations
from Kweisi Mfume, NAACP president and chief executive
officer. "Du Bois's epic work described aspects of an existence too often unrecognized or regarded without sympathy
by the majority of Americans a century ago," Mfume observed. "He also offered empathy for those who oppressed
African-Americans, even while describing the cruelties committed due to the divisiveness of the color-line." The real
goal of Du Bois, according to Mfume, was the achievement
of "mutual respect . . . as a necessary prelude to harmonious coexistence" between racial groups. Du Bois "re-
viled" racial hatred, "but not those who espoused or acted
upon it." Mfume's curious construction made Du Bois seem
more like Martin Luther King Jr. than the author of *Souls*.
Thus, fifty-five years after he was fired from the NAACP,
and forty years after his death in involuntary exile in Ghana,
both Du Bois and his most famous text are comfortably re-
assimilated into the current mission statement of the civil
rights establishment.

What would Du Bois himself have thought about this
multimillion-dollar fête in his honor? How would he have
felt about his portrayal? Being the careful social scientist
that he was, Du Bois would probably ask what was really
being celebrated. There was certainly a superficial famil-
iarity with passages from *Souls* by most of the evening's
speakers, but virtually no mention of the repressive, brutal

context of life under Jim Crow segregation in the South that was the immediate environment of the writing of this collection of essays. The metaphor of the "color-line" provided useful connections with the realities of structural racism in the post–Civil Rights era—the continuing burdens black Americans endure in the form of lower life expectancies, higher infant mortality rates, lower rates of college enrollment and graduation, and higher rates of imprisonment. As I was sitting high above the Talented Tenth, with the night's mantras washing over me with a tidal consistency, I finally understood the deeper meaning of the celebration. Du Bois had given the emerging black middle class a lyrical language of racial reform.

Souls was to the black American petit bourgeoisie what *The Communist Manifesto* had once been for radical sectors of the European proletariat under industrial capitalism in the late nineteenth century: a framework for understanding history. It was a philosophical statement establishing group identity and social location within an unequal society, and also an appeal for collective action and resistance to oppression and exploitation. Unfortunately, from my seat it didn't seem like the black elite, or their corporate sponsors, were much interested in class struggle or in Du Bois's Marxist politics after World War II. The black elite was there largely to celebrate itself and the general advancement of the race within U.S. society. Du Bois was being honored for giving that rising class a language of its own.

While the Detroit NAACP chapter's massive celebration of *Souls* was the largest single event of its kind, there were at least several hundred other such public programs during

the book's centennial year. The most ambitious was sponsored by the National Black Arts Festival in Atlanta in July
2003. Its self-described mission of "Searching for Soul
. . . in all the right places" coyly combined the "spotlight
on W. E. B. Du Bois" with a wide-ranging series of cultural performances and conversations. A number of the
cultural festival's panels did focus on various interpretations of the book and included noted scholars and writers
such as Thulani Davis, Sheila S. Walker, and Richard Long.
Other panels, however, on topics such as "Afro Futurism"
and "Post-Black Visual Arts," seemed to have at best a
slim connection with either *Souls* or Du Bois. Once again,
both local and transnational corporations were on hand to
celebrate Du Bois, and it was only appropriate, since Atlanta has become the South's capital for globalization. A
short list of prominent funders included Coca-Cola, Wachovia Bank, American Express, Lincoln Mercury, Delta
Airlines, AT&T, Georgia Power, Turner Broadcasting Systems, and Altria Corporate Services. Again, I was invited
to give a lecture at the festival, this time on "The Politics
of W. E. B. Du Bois and Global Consciousness." After
talking with one conference planner, I understood that no
exhaustive critique of the text itself or the political context
that had motivated Du Bois in the first place was desired.

   In New York City, several public events honoring *The
Souls of Black Folk* were also arranged. On April 7, 2003,
historian Robin D. G. Kelley participated as a narrator
during dramatic readings of excerpts from *Souls,* staged by
author/playwright Thulani Davis. The dramatic readings

also featured actors Danny Glover, Phylicia Rashad, and Jeffrey Wright. Funds for the event were donated by Trans-Africa Forum, the premier black-American lobby, on behalf of African and Caribbean countries. Harvard's highly esteemed African-American studies program, named in honor of Du Bois, also orchestrated a major event around *Souls*—a series of readings from the text held at Boston's Memorial Church on April 25, 2003. Celebrating "the centennial of the landmark work" were speakers Henry Louis Gates Jr., Michael Dawson, Homi Bhabha, Anthony Appiah, Evelyn Brooks Higginbotham, and Du Bois's stepson, David Graham Du Bois.

What was most significant about this event, however, was Gates's subtle effort to reframe the meaning of both Du Bois and his book. "No one did more to place the American Negro in the world as a full-voiced speaking subject than did W. E. B. Du Bois," Gates observed in his opening remarks. Du Bois must be remembered for two principal contributions, Gates argued, "one political and one literary." Du Bois's major political accomplishment was his role in creating the NAACP and being "one of the fathers of the Civil Rights Movement." His second major contribution was the invention of the literary "metaphors for the black condition" employed throughout *Souls,* which would be incorporated into the work of several generations of African-American writers. Gates's definition of Du Bois as a literary artist and liberal pragmatist effectively cut off from critical discussion the final forty years of Du Bois's public life.

The news media coverage generated by the *Souls* centennial events, just like the public celebrations, emphasized only a few key phrases or ideas expressed in the text. The most prominent was, of course, the most famous sentence Du Bois ever wrote in his long career—"the problem of the twentieth century is the problem of the color-line." "Du Bois could not have known when he wrote these words in 1903 that they'd remain an indelible part of the nation's discussions on race 100 years later," observed Anica Butler in the *Hartford Courant*.

Likewise, Lynne Duke of *The Washington Post* led her story with Du Bois's famous quote, although not to praise it: "Excuse me, sir. I'm looking for the color line. Would you know where I can find it?" Duke claimed that Du Bois's formulation, while true enough a century ago, was an anachronism today. "Since Du Bois's day, the color line has gone undercover. No signs. No laws. No night riders in white sheets. And it's no longer a black-white thing," Duke added to distinguish the rigid racial context of the Jim Crow South from the multicultural, post–Civil Rights America of the twenty-first century. Duke's main point—that immigration and globalization have added "new shades of complexity to the color line"—was fully anticipated by Du Bois and is actually central to his formulation of the problem. The "color-line" for Du Bois was never just black versus white, but was also "the relation of the darker to the lighter races of men in Asia and Africa, in America and the islands of the seas."

Du Bois's theory of double consciousness—that the African-American was simultaneously "an American, a Negro; two souls, two thoughts, two unreconciled strivings"—garnered equal attention and commentary. Another frequently mentioned theme was Du Bois's promulgation of the role of the "Talented Tenth"—college-educated, middle-class African Americans who were expected to lead the uplifting of the race. For *Nashville City Paper* staff writer Ron Wynn, Du Bois was a "role model" who "felt that those blacks who are most gifted—he called them the 'talented tenth'—should not only receive the best training and preparation but also be equally willing to use their newly acquired skills to help others attain freedom." It was a shame, Wynn added, that "Du Bois became so disillusioned at his native land's treatment of African Americans that he renounced his U.S. Citizenship" and died in Ghana.

Wynn's assertion was wrong on several counts. After Du Bois's indictment and subsequent legal vindication in federal court in 1951, the U.S. State Department nevertheless seized his passport and withheld it until 1958. The late Herbert Aptheker, Du Bois's literary executor, explained to me that when Du Bois left the United States to travel to Ghana on October 5, 1961, it was with the expectation that he would eventually return to the United States. In his biography of Du Bois, David Levering Lewis notes that "Du Bois became a citizen of Ghana" on his ninety-fifth birthday "largely because the American embassy refused to renew his passport."

The media also focused on Du Bois's confrontation with black educator Booker T. Washington, the founder of the Tuskegee Institute and the most powerful African-American political leader of the early 1900s. They claimed that Du Bois's bold advocacy of full civil rights and equality for blacks was sharply at odds with the conservative accommodationism of Booker T. Washington. On Tavis Smiley's syndicated radio program on April 17, 2003, two readers portrayed the views of Washington and Du Bois. One widely reprinted United Press International column by Dallas journalist John Bloom grossly oversimplified the positions of both Washington and Du Bois, characterizing "Tuskegeeism" as "training up the black race in trades so they could be of economic value to the nation," with Du Bois holding "the opposite view."

To their credit, many scholars made determined efforts to set the historical record straight—to explain the meaning of Du Bois's work without turning it into what journalist Lynne Duke described as an "almost sacred text." Robin Kelley described Du Bois as "the most important American intellectual to reflect on the meaning of modernity in the Western world, with influence on all aspects of human science." David Levering Lewis correctly characterized Du Bois's commentary on Booker T. Washington as marking "the beginning of the modern civil rights movement," and in various publications cautioned against a narrow, elitist interpretation of what Du Bois meant by the "Talented Tenth."

The most insightful appreciation of Du Bois and *Souls* to appear in the popular press was written by cultural studies scholar Stuart Hall in the *(London) Guardian*. Hall began his essay with the regret that Du Bois's "life and work are, alas, little known on this side of the Atlantic." Du Bois's lasting significance and relevance, Hall suggested, came from "his single-minded commitment to racial justice and his capacity to shape black consciousness." In *Souls,* culture and politics are inextricably linked in the process of group self-awareness and affirmation. "Du Bois used language and ideas to hammer out a strategy for political equality," Hall observed, "and to sound the depths of the black experience in the aftermath of slavery." *The Souls of Black Folk* was the first book that tried to honestly paint for white America "a vivid portrait of black people in the decades after emancipation in 1862—how they lived and who they really were—and thus to enlighten white America—still profoundly attached to myths of black inferiority—as to the true meaning of being black in post–Civil War America."

It is no exaggeration to say that *The Souls of Black Folk* has remained the most influential text about the African-American experience for a century. Even Du Bois's contemporaries, whether agreeing with or dissenting from its arguments, understood its unique power as a work of literature. James Weldon Johnson observed that *Souls* had "a greater effect upon and within the black race in America than any other single book published in this country since *Uncle Tom's Cabin.*" A fuller appreciation of *The Souls of Black Folk* in our own time—more than a generation removed from the enactment of the Civil Rights Act of 1964, which outlawed racial segregation in all public accommodations—requires a reconstruction of the context in which it was produced.

The fourteen essays included in *Souls* were written between 1897 and 1903, the years Du Bois spent developing his social science research projects at Atlanta University, in the heartland of an increasingly segregated and violent South. It was life in the South—where lynchings were fast becoming commonplace and where Du Bois's son died after being denied medical attention by white doctors—that lead Du Bois to question the ability of academic knowledge alone to address the problems facing those who lived behind the veil. Du Bois was eventually forced to confront the human consequences of American structural racism and its effects upon its most marginalized and vulnerable victims. Du Bois's acute sensitivity to Southern injustice provided the impetus for the writing of *Souls,* but it was the enduring lessons from his youth in the North that did much to inform his artful language and poetic passion.

Du Bois was born on February 23, 1868, in Great Barrington, Massachusetts. It was less than three years after the conclusion of the Civil War, and only five years after the Emancipation Proclamation. Upon graduation from high school he was enrolled at Fisk University in Nashville, Tennessee. The experience at Fisk gave the young Du Bois his first real understanding of African-American culture and life in the rural South. In *Souls* Du Bois describes with loving attention his trials as a schoolteacher in rural Tennessee. Completing his bachelor's degree, Du Bois transferred to Harvard College, where he was admitted to start his junior year. In 1890 he was awarded his BA degree cum laude from Harvard, and he first came to public attention as a commencement speaker at his graduation ceremony. He selected for his oration the provocative topic of Jefferson Davis, the former president of the Confederacy. His balanced description of Davis as "the peculiar champion of a people fighting to be free in order that another people should not be free" was widely praised as fair. *The Nation* noted with approval that the "slender, intellectual-looking mulatto" had "handled his difficult and hazardous subject with absolute good taste, great moderation and almost contemptuous fairness."

Du Bois pursued his graduate studies at Harvard, and with the financial support of a scholarship from the Slater Fund he attended the University of Berlin and traveled extensively throughout Europe from 1892 to 1894. Awarded a Ph.D. in history from Harvard in 1895, his dissertation, "The Suppression of the African Slave-Trade to the United States of America, 1638–1870," was published the following year as the initial volume in the Harvard Historical Studies Series. Despite being the first African American to receive a Ph.D. from Harvard University, he was not offered employment at any white academic institution. He taught briefly at Wilberforce University, a historically black college in Ohio, and from 1896 to 1897 was employed by the University of Pennsylvania to conduct a social survey of Philadelphia's black community. The product of this study, *The Philadelphia Negro*, was the first social science examination of race and racism in an urban context. In 1897, Du Bois received an appointment as professor of history and economics at Atlanta University, where he immediately launched an ambitious series of annual research conferences dedicated to the study of the American Negro.

Aside from Du Bois's scholarly productivity during these years, he was extensively involved in civic activities and international efforts to build a pan-Africanist movement, and he made frequent journalistic forays into public debates. In 1897, Du Bois along with noted scholar Alexander Crummell and other black intellectuals established the American Negro Academy, the first black academic society in the United States. The objective of the American Negro Academy—to encourage a cultural and intellectual renaissance among blacks in America—in many ways anticipated the Harlem Renaissance of the 1920s. Working with Trinidadian barrister Henry Sylvester Williams, Du Bois helped organize the first Pan-African Conference in London in August 1900, initiating a global process that would culminate half a century later in powerful independence movements across Africa and the Caribbean.

All of these wide-ranging intellectual endeavors occurred at a time of extreme political repression for African Americans. Several hundred blacks were lynched annually in the South throughout the 1890s. In 1896, the U.S. Supreme Court in its *Plessy v. Ferguson* decision established the legality of the "separate but equal" standard, which justified racial segregation in public accommodations, schools, and nearly all other aspects of public life. In 1890 Mississippi took the lead in disfranchising its black electorate, and other Southern states soon followed. By the early 1900s, local ordinances had been adopted that created two parallel racial universes separating black and white Americans. Blacks could not run for elective office and in most cases were denied the right to vote. They were not permitted to attend whites-only schools, or to patronize whites-only restrooms, restaurants, and hotels. They were even refused access to white hospitals. Blacks would soon be excluded from juries, and would be denied admission to theatres and other public amusements except in racially segregated seating sections.

It was against this brutal background of white supremacy and black subordination that Booker T. Washington emerged as a national spokesman on the issues of race. In 1881 Washington established Tuskegee Institute in Alabama's Black Belt. By 1900, the Tuskegee Institute was the largest postsecondary school for Negroes in the world. Washington was catapulted to national attention in September 1895 when he delivered a short address at the Cotton States and International Exposition in Atlanta. In this speech, later described as the Atlanta Compromise, Washington appeared to surrender any overt claim to voting and equal rights for African Americans. He seemed to accept the reality of racial segregation, declaring that "in all things that are purely social we can be as separate as the fingers, yet one as the hand in all things essential to mutual progress." In return African Americans would expect opportunities for land ownership, business development, and vocational training in the South. Washington urged blacks to build their own institutions for creating and distributing goods and services for black consumers, utilizing racial segregation as a buffer to sustain a separate economy. Washington's pragmatic approach to segregation appealed to many African-American small business owners, farmers, and educators in industrial training schools.

For decades in black American political culture, the legend of the powerful ideological struggle between Booker T. Washington and W. E. B. Du Bois has grown and hardened.

In truth, Du Bois was not at first in sharp disagreement with the "Wizard of Tuskegee," as Washington was occasionally described by his supporters. Days after Washington delivered the Atlanta Compromise address, Du Bois sent him a glowing note of congratulations for his "phenomenal success in Atlanta—it was a word fitly spoken." Du Bois worried about criticisms of Washington that soon appeared in the African-American press, and he promptly forwarded a letter to the *New York Age* in the Tuskegeean's defense. Washington's controversial proposal, Du Bois believed, "might be the basis of a real settlement between whites and blacks in the South, if the South opened to the Negroes the doors of economic opportunity and the Negroes co-operated with the South in political sympathy."

Washington reciprocated these gestures of friendship and esteem. In early 1900, the position of superintendent of Washington, D.C.'s Negro schools was advertised, and although Du Bois did not actively seek the appointment, Washington pushed for him. In a letter dated March 11, 1900, Washington informed the black scholar that he had "recommended" him "as strongly as I could." In the summer of 1901, Du Bois and his family were invited to be houseguests at Washington's West Virginia residence. In July 1902, Washington praised Du Bois's scholarship on the state of black public schools in the South.

In his 1944 essay, "My Evolving Program for Negro Freedom," Du Bois recalled that he "was not overcritical of Booker T. Washington" during these years. Du Bois wrote that in 1902 he met with Washington privately to discuss the possibility of leaving Atlanta University and transferring his various research projects to Tuskegee Institute. "If I had been offered a chance at Tuskegee to pursue my program of investigation, with larger funds and opportunity, I would doubtless have accepted," Du Bois later admitted.

Ideologically and even in terms of public policy, Du Bois and Washington were not far apart. Washington emphasized the importance of practical vocational training for Negroes, 90 percent of whom lived in rural areas and worked mostly in agriculture. Similarly, Du Bois viewed colleges and industrial schools as complementary, and he always acknowledged the significant role of trade schools and vocational training for black advancement. In 1901, Du Bois publicly applauded Tuskegee Institute's decade-long campaign against the worst effects of the sharecropping system on the black community. On the issue of black business development, both men were largely in accord. Du Bois strongly favored black entrepreneurship as a sign of the race's growing capacity for self-sufficiency. In his 1898 speech on the meaning of business, Du Bois preached that African Americans had to accumulate capital and invest it constructively. "The day the Negro race courts and marries the savings-bank," Du Bois predicted, "will be the day of its salvation." Washington was for all practical purposes the "father of black capitalism"—founder of the National Negro Business League, proponent of black entrepreneurship, and advocate of black property ownership.

Based on the historical evidence, then, it is a mistake to judge the Washington–Du Bois conflict as inevitable. Most of the militant black intellectuals and political activists who took public positions against Washington's policies of accommodation, such as Boston *Guardian* editor William Monroe Trotter and crusading antilynching journalist Ida B. Wells-Barnett, did not consider Du Bois a "radical." In July 1902, for example, Trotter complained to his friends that Du Bois was not to be trusted or relied on in the struggle against Washington.

A small publishing house in Chicago, A. C. McClurg and Company, contacted Du Bois in 1902 to ask if he had any material that could be published as a book. Du Bois wanted to produce "a social study which should be perhaps a summing up of the work of the Atlanta Conferences, or at any rate, a scientific investigation," he wrote later in *Dusk of Dawn*. But McClurg suggested a volume of collected essays. "I demurred," Du Bois later wrote, "because books of essays almost always fall so flat. Nevertheless, I got together a number of my fugitive pieces." Although the essays he selected for *Souls* had been written over a period of seven years, designed originally for very different audiences and covering a broad range of topics, they nevertheless had many things in common.

As Farah Jasmine Griffin has observed, one central element was "Du Bois's consistent use of the first person, his insertion of himself as a subjective student and participant in black life and culture." In several previously published essays, Du Bois had already developed the effective metaphor of the veil to represent the structural barriers between the black and white worlds. His repeated references to the veil helped bring a thematic coherence to the new work. As Griffin notes, in most of the essays "Du Bois turns to academic fields of knowledge such as history, sociology, and philosophy to assist in his interpretation of the complexity of black lives. While these fields help to provide the framework for his analysis, his prose is shaped by biblical and mythological narrative, metaphor and allusion."

What is most striking to me about *Souls* as a political statement is the moderate nature of its tone. If Du Bois had not included "Of Mr. Booker T. Washington and Others," the essay that explicitly criticized the Tuskegee agenda, *Souls* would have been essentially the same book in its contents, but would probably not have been perceived or remembered as a radical challenge to Jim Crow. In his essay "Of the Sons of Master and Man," for instance, Du Bois carefully draws out the logical reasons why most Southern whites feared the extension of equal rights to African Americans. In language remarkably similar to Washington's, Du Bois called upon Southern whites and blacks alike to set aside their prejudices—"to see and appreciate and sympathize with each other's position for the Negro to realize more deeply than he does at present the need of uplifting the masses of his people, for white people to realize more vividly than they have yet done the deadening and disastrous effect of . . . color prejudice." Interracial progress is possible, Du Bois suggested, "only by a union of intelligence and sympathy across the color-line." These don't necessarily sound like the words of a radical, and out of context could easily be mistaken for Washington.

As the manuscript was being prepared for shipment to the publisher, Du Bois made the final decision to insert the essay entitled "Of Booker T. Washington and Others." Nearly forty years later, Du Bois explained that he had become "increasingly uncomfortable" with Washington's position, and was especially troubled by Washington's "general attitude which seemed to place the onus of the blame for the status of Negroes upon the Negroes themselves rather than upon the whites." Yet we now know, from the private correspondence of both, that they continued to cooperate with each other at this time. Washington privately offered his assistance to Du Bois, for example, in pursuing legal action against the Pullman Company for racial discrimination. Only months prior to the publication of *Souls,* Washington and Du Bois came together publicly to denounce the exclusion of blacks from consideration as candidates for Rhodes scholarships in the Atlanta area. In early May 1903, just as the newly printed *Souls* was being shipped to bookstores, Du Bois was preparing to teach summer school at Tuskegee Institute, where he was living on campus.

I strongly suspect that Du Bois did not anticipate that his measured words—what he considered constructive criticism—would be interpreted as a complete rupture from Tuskegee. In the controversial essay, Du Bois characterized Washington as "certainly the most distinguished Southerner since Jefferson Davis, and the one with the largest personal following." The essay called upon "the black men of America" to oppose only "part of the work of their greatest leader. So far as Mr. Washington preaches Thrift, Patience, and Industrial Training for the Masses, we must hold up his hands and strive with him. . . . But so far as Mr. Washington apologizes for injustice, North or South, does not rightly value the privilege and duty of voting, belittles the emasculating effects of caste distinctions. . . we must unceasingly and firmly oppose them."

Nothing Du Bois had previously written prepared him for the avalanche of public reaction generated by *The Souls of Black Folk*. One of the earliest reviews appeared in the April 18, 1903, issue of Trotter's *Guardian,* entitled "Souls of Black Folk: A Great Book by a Great Scholar; Touching the Spiritual Life of Colored People." The *Guardian* praised Du Bois for writing "with the eloquence of a poet, with the foresight of a prophet, with the vigor of a reformer, and with the power only he can possess who has thought deeply upon the wrongs of his own people." The *Guardian* review emphasized Du Bois's critique of Washington: "In his consideration of that modern movement of which Mr. Booker T. Washington is the leader, Mr. Du Bois speaks strongly of the man who he believes is striving for much and accomplishing but little."

Within days of the *Guardian*'s glowing tribute to *Souls,* there appeared a sharply negative and boldly racist review in *The New York Times.* "It is generally conceded that Booker T. Washington represents the best hope of the negro in America," the review began. Du Bois clearly "does not understand his own people in their natural state as does [Washington]." Equally brutal was a review in the *Colored American,* a newspaper closely aligned with Washington, accusing Du Bois of being simply a "hanger-on at a place created by white people." The reviewer complained that Du Bois's inclusion of the essay critical of Washington in his volume was an opportunistic publicity stunt, because *The Souls of Black Folk* would have found few readers on "its own bottom."

A number of the early reviews followed the lead of *The New York Times* and roundly condemned Du Bois, focusing primarily on two issues—his criticisms of Washington and his opposition to racial segregation and disfranchisement. The *Outlook*'s May 23, 1903, issue misinterpreted Du Bois's double-consciousness theory as meaning that "the negro and the American are ever separate, though in the same personality. . . . The sense of amused contempt and pity for his own race, caught from the white people, is reflected in the title of Professor Du Bois's book, 'The Souls of the Black Folk.'" The differences between Du Bois and Washington reflected two divergent "influences in the negro race. . . . One of these parties is ashamed of the race, the other is proud of it . . . one wishes to teach the negro to read the Ten Commandments in Hebrew; the other wishes first to teach him to obey them in English."

The review of *Souls* appearing in the July 1903 issue of the *South Atlantic Quarterly* correctly interpreted the veil metaphor, but then praised Washington for embracing racial segregation and for "glorify[ing] the negro race until it shall be no dishonor to be black. Du Bois would chafe and fret, and tear his heart out. And as for us, who are a divinely appointed superior race, how much do we do to render the burden lighter to either the one or the other?" The reviewer, John Spencer Basset, who edited the *South Atlantic Quarterly*, acknowledged that "Du Bois's protest is not a violent one. It is a cry of a man who suffers. . . . [I]t bears the evidence that its author while he was writing realized the hopelessness of it all." The *American Monthly Review of Reviews* suggested that *Souls* "deserves a wide reading," but not for the accuracy of its views. "Professor Du Bois is a man of the highest culture, and he cannot overcome the sensitiveness natural to a man of fine feelings placed in the position he occupies. . . . The result is truly pathetic."

Despite such negative reviews, public demand for *Souls* was strong, and A. C. McClurg and Company subsequently ordered a second and a third printing. As the book circulated nationally, it attracted reviews from more liberal publications, which immediately recognized the significance of Du Bois's accomplishment. *The Nation*'s June 11, 1903, issue announced that "Du Bois has written a profoundly interesting and affecting book, remarkable as a piece of literature apart from its inner significance." Most surprising to *The Nation* was the power of the author's passion reflected throughout the text. Those "who have heard Mr. Du Bois speak," and found him "coldly intellectual, have not been at all prepared for the emotion and the passion throbbing here in every chapter, almost every page. It is almost intolerably sad."

The *Congregationalist and Christian World* applauded *Souls* as "almost the first fully articulate voice from what the author calls 'the veil'—the full expression of the soul of a people. It does not matter that Professor Du Bois is Massachusetts born; long years of work among his fellow Negroes in the South have given him a right to speak for the children of the slaves in their difficult effort to make real a race aspiration in the face of a higher and hostile environment." This reviewer also agreed with Du Bois's balanced criticisms of Washington, adding, "We are not ready to admit that the higher education of the Negro has been a failure."

The New York *Independent* observed that Du Bois's book "makes plain" the "pitiful injustice—industrial, political, and social—meted out to the negro by his lords and masters of the Anglo-Saxon race in America." The Los Angeles publication *Outwest* praised *Souls* as an "eloquent and penetrating discussion" of American race relations. "The voice of a man, lifted to tell unstutteringly those truths concerning life which burn hottest in his own heart, is always worth an attentive ear. The *Outwest* reviewer added, "And if the voice be both trained and melodious, its utterances are, in the finest sense, Literature. *The Souls of Black Folk* falls, without possibility of dispute, under this category."

How did Du Bois respond to this sudden explosion of interest in his work, and to both the praises and bitter criticisms *Souls* had provoked? One excellent insight is provided by a lengthy interview with the author that appeared in the June 16, 1903, *Chicago Daily Tribune,* under the headline, "Cultured Negro Model for Race." The *Tribune* reporter, "Raymond," described an evening spent with Du Bois, depicting the scene at Atlanta University in vivid detail: "After trudging up two flights of stairs, through bare, uncarpeted halls, one suddenly finds himself transported into the busy literary workshop of a close student. Seated at the center of a big table, revolving easily in his office chair, alert, intelligent, conservative, weighing his words cautiously, and yet speaking with the confidence born of profound study, the picture of this brown-skinned, well-dressed, self-poised scholar was not soon to be forgotten."

Du Bois expressed surprise at the public attention focusing on *Souls,* the *Tribune* reporter explained, "because he was the author of many other works which he believes more important." The interview focused largely on Du Bois's general views about the state of race relations, the benefits of higher education for Negroes, and the link between political and economic power. Du Bois did not directly mention Washington, but the reporter could not avoid the obvious differences between the two men. "Professor Du Bois believes that the salvation of his race must come through the exercise of the right of franchise as the necessary preliminary to commercial equality," the *Tribune* reporter concluded. "The line of cleavage between this element of Negroes and that represented by Booker T. Washington is daily becoming more marked, and this is a pity, because two such men as Du Bois and Washington, undoubtedly the brainiest of their race, ought to be brought together to work more in harmony for the ultimate uplifting of their own people."

Of the great number of articles assigned to review *The Souls of Black Folk,* many simply ignored the contents of the book and speculated about the growing ideological controversy between Washington and Du Bois. The *(London) Times Literary Supplement* of August 14, 1903, described *Souls* as "an extraordinary compound of emotion and statistics, of passionate revolt and sober restraint." But the real question worth pursuing, the reviewer suggested, was what *Souls* represented in regard to the future of black leadership in America. "There are, it seems, two schools of thought among educated Negroes: the one, led by Mr. Booker Washington, would abandon the struggle for political power and higher education and pursue the conciliation of the South and the acquisition of wealth; the other, headed by the present author, would break down the color prejudice by higher education and civil rights." This reviewer then made what was, in retrospect, a remarkable prediction: "If there should ever arise a leader of the caliber of Professor Du Bois who could command the allegiance of all educated negroes, events more dramatic than the gradual decay of color-prejudice might come to pass."

As newspapers, magazines, and journals covered *Souls*, liberal and reform-minded scholars and activists, both black and white, discussed and debated the book's central ideas. In early May 1903, a forum to discuss *Souls* was held in Chicago. It included Tuskegee Institute Professor Monroe Work, journalist Ida B. Wells-Barnett, and her husband Ferdinand Barnett, the first African-American assistant state's attorney in Illinois. On May 30, Ida Wells-Barnett wrote to Du Bois about the forum, observing that "we are still reading your book with the same delighted appreciation." From the British West African colony of the Gold Coast, attorney and author Casely Hayford sent a letter of congratulations to Du Bois: "I have recently had the pleasure of reading your great work, 'The Souls of Black Folk,' and it occurred to me if leading thinkers of the African race in America had the opportunity of exchanging thoughts with the thinkers of the African race in West Africa, this century would be likely to see the race problem solved." Prominent German social scientist Max Weber contacted Du Bois, insisting that his "splendid work . . . ought *to be translated into German*" [Weber's emphasis]. Weber proposed a suitable translator for the task, and then offered "to write a short introduction about the Negro question and literature and should be much obligated to you for some information about your life, viz: age, birthplace, descent, positions held by you—of course only *if you give your authorization*" [Weber's emphasis].

At this time Du Bois was receiving not only letters from academics and prospective foreign allies but also fan mail. A young African-American woman in her junior year of undergraduate studies at Cornell University, Jessie Fauset, sent to Du Bois on December 26, 1903, a letter of appreciation for *Souls*: "I am glad, glad you wrote it—we have needed someone to voice the intricacies of the blind maze of thought and action along which the modern, educated colored man or woman struggles. It hurt you to write that book, didn't it? The man of fine sensibilities has to suffer exquisitely, just simply because his feeling is so fine."

It would take a year or more for Du Bois to fully appreciate what *The Souls of Black Folk* had set into motion. In a revealing short essay in the *Independent,* published in November 1904, Du Bois reflected critically about *Souls* and the unexpected storm of controversy it had created. He explained that he had deliberately employed throughout the text "a personal and intimate tone of self-revelation. In each essay I sought to speak from within—to depict a world as we see it who dwell therein." Then in a remarkable passage that seemingly repudiated the double-consciousness theory, Du Bois mused: "In its larger aspects the style is tropical—African. This needs no apology. The blood of my fathers spoke through me and cast off the English restraint of my training and surroundings. The resulting accomplishment is a matter of taste. Sometimes I think very well of it and sometimes I do not."

Few books make history, and fewer still become foundational texts for the movements and struggles of an entire people. *The Souls of Black Folk* occupies this rare position. It helped to create the intellectual argument for the black freedom struggle in the twentieth century. *Souls* justified the pursuit of higher education for Negroes and thus contributed to the rise of the black middle class. By describing a global color-line, Du Bois anticipated pan-Africanism and colonial revolutions in the Third World. Moreover, this stunning critique of how "race" is lived through the normal aspects of daily life is central to what would become known as "whiteness studies" a century later.

Yet Du Bois's central role as the architect and chief theoretician of the early NAACP, and as bold advocate of an integrated American society, gave the emerging African-American middle strata, his "Talented Tenth," the language for the struggles of racial reform. Over time, Du Bois realized that racial justice in America would require profound structural change within the U.S. political economy; his "Talented Tenth" had not yet reached those conclusions about their own politics.

From the original publication of *Souls* in 1903 until his resignation from the editorship of the NAACP's magazine, the *Crisis*, in 1934, no one in America personified the struggle for racial justice more than Du Bois. Even during the difficult years of the Great Depression and the Second World War, when Du Bois was employed again at Atlanta University and without a political organization or public policy platform, he continued to be widely recognized as the most important intellectual of the entire black world. Well into his 60s and 70s, Du Bois attempted to shape black public opinion through a newspaper column appearing in the African-American press. He produced in 1935, at the age of 67, what is arguably his finest work, *Black Reconstruction*. It was only after 1945, with the onset of the anticommunist hysteria of the Cold War, that Du Bois's status as an icon of the civil rights cause came under fire.

The process of subverting the intellectual and political legacy of Du Bois started even prior to Du Bois's death in 1963. The Cold War liberals who exercised domination over the scholarship related to the Negro and to race relations always had an extremely difficult time relating to Du Bois. It was only partially due to the depths of their anticommunism, and to their outrage that Du Bois had become identified with what a later president would term, the "evil empire." For scholars such as early Du Bois biographer Francis L. Broderick, their greatest dilemma was that Du Bois failed to conform or fit into the arbitrary categories they had constructed to analyze patterns of African-American social thought and black political culture. To minimize Du Bois's legacy, they questioned the

value and even the legitimacy of the bulk of his scholarship. They ridiculed Du Bois's various political shifts and
tactical oscillations between integrationism and black nationalism. They criticized his austere personality as cold,
aloof, and isolated from genuine human interaction and
social contacts. Their ultimate objective was to bury, once
and for all, the contributions of Du Bois, Paul Robeson,
Harlem Councilman Benjamin Davis, and other African-
American radicals who had been identified with Marxist
socialism. If the Negro was to be "freed," in their judgment, it would be under the banner of American democracy and U.S. capitalism.

One of Du Bois's harshest Cold War–era critics in the
early sixties was Harold Isaacs. During the 1930s, Isaacs
had been active in the deeply anticommunist Trotskyist
movement. In 1950, the Trotskyist Socialist Workers Party
ran a candidate, Joseph Hansen, against Du Bois during his
unsuccessful campaign for the United States Senate in New
York. During the campaign, Hansen repeatedly accused
Du Bois of "permitting the local agents of the Kremlin police regime to exploit your good name and distinguished
reputation for reactionary ends." Although Isaacs had officially distanced himself from the Trotskyist left by the early
1960s, its polemic views still influenced his general interpretation of black American leaders like Du Bois. Isaacs's
1963 book, *The New World of Negro Americans,* which
received the Anisfield-Wolf Award given to the best book
on U.S. race relations, pilloried Du Bois on a wide variety
of grounds. For Isaacs, Du Bois was simply a pompous
"breakfast-table autocrat" whose "half-digested Marxism"

and elitism had culminated "in a close embrace–indeed a marriage–with totalitarian Communist world power." Reviewing Du Bois's entire intellectual output and public career, Isaacs found grievous shortcomings and errors of all types. He claimed that Du Bois's Pan-African Congresses were "unsuccessful" and represented little more than "romantic racism." Isaacs concluded that "other Negroes have been far greater as leaders and played much larger historic roles," and stressed that "Du Bois is hardly to be classed as a world shaker or world changer."

Ultimately, it was the black freedom movement of the 1960s, rather than the enlightenment of mainstream social science research on issues of race, that was largely responsible for the fundamental reevaluation and rehabilitation of Du Bois's intellectual and political reputation. Most key civil rights activists of the time had read and were very familiar with Du Bois's ideas. As historian Gerald Horne relates, Student Nonviolent Coordinating Committee organizers James Forman and H. Rap Brown both acknowledged being directly influenced by Du Bois. Only weeks before Dr. Martin Luther King Jr.'s 1968 assassination, he praised Du Bois before a Carnegie Hall gathering. "History cannot ignore W. E. B. Du Bois," King declared. "It is time to cease muting the fact that Dr. Du Bois was a genius that chose to be a Communist."

With the sudden emergence of Black Power and of African-American studies as an interdisciplinary field of scholarship and research at predominantly white academic institutions, awareness of Du Bois's intellectual legacy increased dramatically. In Atlanta, for example, when dozens of African-American studies department directors caucused in November 1969 to map a strategy for the development of their field, they consciously drew upon Du Bois's intellectual heritage. As historian Vincent Harding has related, the 1969 establishment of the Institute of the Black World, an independent African-American research center, was precisely to fulfill Du Bois's intellectual vision. "Based as we were in Atlanta," Harding noted later, "it was not difficult for us to remember and recount his work at the beginning of the century toward a research center which would develop a hundred-year study of the Black Experience."

The 1970s and 1980s witnessed the full flowering of what could be termed Du Boisian scholarship. Leading the way were black intellectuals such as Gerald Horne, whose 1986 *Black and Red* was an outstanding analysis of Du Bois's career from 1944 until his death in 1963. Others at the vanguard of Du Boisian scholarship were Cedric Robinson, author of *Black Marxism* and *Black Movements in America,* and Arnold Rampersad, who published *The Art and Imagination of W. E. B. Du Bois* in 1976. Hundreds of scholarly articles and several dozen dissertations were produced in these years examining Du Bois's contributions in the social sciences, humanities, and arts. None of these works would have been possible, of course, without the monumental sacrifices and labors of Marxist historian Herbert Aptheker. Aptheker's three-volume, closely annotated *Correspondence of W. E. B. Du Bois (1973–1978),* his edited versions of Du Bois's writings that appeared in hundreds of periodicals and edited volumes, and his 1973 *Annotated Bibliography* of Du Bois's complete *oeuvre* established the intellectual foundations for all future scholarship and subsequent treatments of Du Bois.

By the Reagan era, much of the intellectual architecture that supported black social movements was becoming more consciously Du Boisian. One prominent example during these years was Jesse Jackson's 1984 presidential campaign, which was constructed around a broad multiracial, left, social democratic-oriented constituency called the Rainbow Coalition. In *The Rainbow Challenge,* Sheila Collins, a field organizer and then national officer in the 1984 campaign, observed that Du Bois's famous double consciousness formulation from *The Souls of Black Folk* had embodied, from a theoretical and philosophical perspective, the ultimate aims of Jackson's effort:

> The Jackson campaign can be interpreted as the black community's effort to work out, on the plane of national politics, the merger of its two warring selves. The campaign functioned, therefore, as a psychological therapeutic process for the African-American community. But it was more than just a cathartic experience. . . . Precisely because it attempted to merge a critique of American society from the perspective of the African-American experience with the seldom-fulfilled ideals embodied in core American political institutions, the Jackson campaign offered the American people a unique opportunity to turn the nation in the direction of peace, justice, and true internationalism.

Collins emphasized that Du Bois's advocacy of pan-Africanism and Third World liberation also helped shape the Jackson campaign's approach to contemporary international policy issues. Again citing *The Souls of Black Folk* for its linkage of black American consciousness with the struggles of other oppressed nonwestern people, Collins noted, "It was this sense of kinship with the oppressed, more than any utilitarian calculation of interests, that determined both the Jackson campaign's outreach to specific constituencies, and its stance on foreign policy."

By the late 1980s the originality and significance of Du Bois's theoretical formulations and social observations were largely unchallenged. Indeed, when compared to the historical writings of white American or European left intellectuals about matters such as race, the underdevelopment of nonwestern societies, or even the dynamics of imperialism, the scholarly consensus was that Du Bois came out well ahead. For example, Paul Buhle's 1987 *Marxism in the United States* placed Du Bois at the center of the theoretical legacy of American Marxism. For Buhle, Du Bois's rich theoretical insights transcended "the limits of every Marxism . . . including Leninism as it had been understood." At the base of Du Bois's magnificent study, *Black Reconstruction,* Buhle asserted, was the explosive assertion that the failure of U.S. labor forces to embrace the struggle to challenge racism had been an international calamity. Unlike most of the older Marxist historical interpretations that treated blacks as passive victims of a voracious bourgeoisie, Du Bois looked to African Americans as active agents in the construction of America's historic narrative.

The 1980s also marked the emergence of an important and insightful black feminist scholarship about the Du Bois legacy. For example, in *Women, Race and Class,* published in 1981, Angela Y. Davis observed: "As a male advocate of woman suffrage, W. E. B. Du Bois was peerless among Black and white men alike. His militancy, his eloquence and the principled character of his numerous appeals caused many of his contemporaries to view him as the most outstanding male defender of women's political equality of his time." Particularly unusual, added Davis, was the "relative lack of male supremacist undertones" that characterized his eloquent appeals. To Davis, Du Bois was one of the few black American male leaders who had fully championed the leadership and full participation of African-American women in virtually every aspect of civic and public life. A similar interpretation of Du Bois was presented in Paula Giddings's widely read 1984 popular history of black women, *When and Where I Enter,* which quoted Du Bois extensively. Nearly all of Giddings's references to Du Bois were highly positive, with few exceptions.

However, as black feminist thought matured in the late 1980s, Du Bois's record of gender politics came under closer scrutiny. In 1987, Mary Ellen Washington criticized the exclusion of black women from the American Negro Academy, formed in 1897 by Alexander Crummell, Du Bois, and others. "This egregious example of sexism in the black intellectual community," Washington noted, "underscores an attitude toward black women that has helped to maintain and perpetuate a male-dominated literary and critical tradition."

Nellie Y. McKay's insightful 1990 essay, "The Souls of Black Women Folk in the Writings of W. E. B. Du Bois," presented a rich critique of the role of gender within the black scholar's work. McKay felt that Du Bois's auto-biographical writings "break out of standard patriarchal paradigms," in part due to the fact that he appeared to understand "the political impact of gender on the lives of black women in America, beginning when he was a young man." However, McKay also found it strange that Du Bois rarely wrote in a meaningful way about his first wife of fifty-three years, Nina Gomer Du Bois. What was certain was that "the marriage was never a union of equals," McKay noted. Nevertheless, despite these obvious limitations in Du Bois's personal life, McKay concluded, "it was in the souls of black women folk that he touched the chords in himself that brought him closest to an understanding of just what that term might mean."

As black feminist scholars reconstructed the history of black knowledge production, they increasingly reached the conclusion that the voices and pivotal contributions of African-American women intellectuals had clearly been suppressed and in some cases obliterated from black history's pages. Although Du Bois had been a contemporary of Anna Julia Cooper, Victoria Mathews, Fannie Barrier Williams, and Ida B. Wells-Barnett, there is relatively little indication in his collective writings and correspondence that he made serious attempts to engage black women intellectuals as equals, or promoted their political influence or ideas. Literary scholar Shirley Wilson Logan noted that the classic turn-of-the-century debate over priorities in black education that were "most often associated with Booker T. Washington and W. E. B. Du Bois" could be viewed and interpreted quite differently through the lens of black women's experiences in the field of education. Logan cited the example of educator Lucy Wilmot Smith, who in 1886, many years prior to Du Bois, "stressed the need to educate hand as well as head, a need she argued was as important for young women as for young men."

In the mid-1980s, amidst the resurgent environment of African-American political resistance to Reaganism, African-American historian David Levering Lewis decided to produce a comprehensive biography of Du Bois. A well-known and widely respected scholar, Lewis had authored a number of works, including *When Harlem Was in Vogue,* published in 1981. Lewis's original objective was to produce a single volume life history. However, given the remarkable breadth and complexity of Du Bois's career, Lewis soon concluded that a two-volume study was necessary, with a logical break point in 1919, following the conclusion of the First World War.

In 1919 Du Bois was fifty-one years old, at the pinnacle of political influence in liberal circles. He was regularly speaking through the NAACP's journal, *The Crisis,* to over 100,000 subscribers and to millions of other Americans through a steady stream of provocative essays, books, and public lectures. Lewis's first volume, *W. E. B. Du Bois: Biography of a Race, 1868–1919,* set out to tell of this remarkable rise to power and intellectual influence. A meticulous scholar, Lewis was at his best in his efforts to correct previous errors and inaccuracies by Du Bois and others in explaining the decisions and details of his life story. This was especially the case in Lewis's sensitive and insightful reading of Du Bois's childhood, teenage years, and early adulthood.

By the time that Lewis's first biographical volume was published in the mid–1990s, the racial climate in the United States had swung to the right once more. Conservative Republicans had seized power in the U.S. Congress, pushing their "contract with America." Affirmative action policies were under fire in courts and legislatures. Within black American politics, the NAACP experienced a near-meltdown, as internal leadership struggles during the brief tenure of National Secretary Benjamin Chavis threatened the group's existence.

Meanwhile, Nation of Islam leader Louis Farrakhan astutely filled the leadership vacuum in black politics, calling for a "Million Man March" mobilization of African-American males in Washington, D.C., in October 1995. This black nationalist–inspired public demonstration had stressed the importance of voting and civic participation, but it had also given greater emphasis to socially conservative themes such as personal responsibility, patriarchal family values, and "moral atonement" that paralleled conservative Republican social policy. Farrakhan had emerged from the success of the Million Man March mobilization as arguably the most influential spokesperson in black America.

The NAACP, desperately seeking to restore its credibility and flagging influence, used to its advantage its own rich history. Myrlie Evers-Williams, noted civil rights activist, was elected as the NAACP's national chairman in 1995.

Evers-Williams personified the association's heroic period of struggle against Jim Crow segregation, and she inspired confidence in the continuing viability of the group.

In a similar fashion, the image and words of Du Bois, once scorned and repudiated by the NAACP, were increasingly rehabilitated. The success of Lewis's book probably influenced this "Du Boisian restoration." For instance, NAACP activist Julian Bond, who two years later would succeed Evers-Williams as the association's national chair, frequently emphasized the Du Boisian legacy's relevance to contemporary civil rights struggles. Writing in an introduction to a denunciatory biography of Farrakhan in 1996, Bond described Du Bois's "prescription for action" as pursuing civil rights and political strength, "seeking coalitions, fighting for entry into the American mainstream." Bond argued that the black nationalist vision represented by "Louis Farrakhan represents an alternative to Du Bois's integrationist vision. He is Du Bois's opposite. The degree of acceptance [Farrakhan] has received says much about the failure of the American dream." While I agree that Du Bois certainly would have never joined the Nation of Islam, it is clear that those who now favored Farrakhan would have embraced enthusiastically Du Bois's concept of the black separatist cooperative economy that he advocated during the Great Depression, along with his active pursuit of pan-Africanism. To suggest that Farrakhan was "Du Bois's opposite" was overly simplistic at best.

When Lewis's second volume, *W. E. B. Du Bois: The Fight for Equality and the American Century, 1919–1963*, finally appeared in 2000, the second Cold War had been over for more than a decade, the Soviet Union had ceased to exist, and Communist China had been transformed into an aggressively capitalist economy. Conservatives—black and white alike—now found it possible to use the figure of Du Bois for the purpose of discrediting and isolating the progressive African-American intelligentsia. "In black intellectual circles, Du Bois is an icon," wrote cultural studies scholar Gerald Early in William F. Buckley's ultraconservative *National Review* in December 2000. "For Columbia's Manning Marable and Harvard scholars Henry Louis Gates and Cornel West, Du Bois is the ideal 'scholar-activist,' the heroic paradigm for African-American academics who describe themselves as engaged intellectuals challenging the very structure that supports them, as other Western intellectuals have done."

For Early, however, this group of intellectuals had failed to recognize that the Du Boisian "legacy is decidedly mixed, as imprisoning as it has been liberating." Early wrote that in *W. E. B. Du Bois: The Fight for Equality*, "among the intellectual failings Lewis points out is Du Bois's tendency, shared by many black intellectuals, today, to romanticize a certain type of authoritarian power, particularly if it is anti-American."

Lewis's second volume, which again received a Pulitzer Prize in biography, presented on balance a much less attractive personality than his first book. Mainstream liberals and conservatives, white and black alike, were largely persuaded by Lewis's critical interpretation of Du Bois. Historian Alan Brinkley, for example, generously praised "Lewis's extraordinary biography." While Du Bois "was undeniably brilliant, a gifted writer and orator," Brinkley noted, he "was never willing to settle for less than complete victory; and over time his definition of victory grew increasingly expansive." Consequently, Du Bois was not only "a poor politician" and "famously arrogant," but represented a political viewpoint that "very early became considerably more radical than anything that the majority of the African-American elite could accept." Brinkley also agreed with Lewis's harsh judgments about Du Bois's gravitation toward revolutionary Marxism: "He was seldom fully in step with his time, and his congenital dissatisfaction with the world he knew led him at times into positions that now seem politically foolish and even morally abhorrent."

Left-liberal and progressive black intellectuals resisted the political decontextualization of Du Bois, and as a group were far more critical of Lewis's second volume than the first. Historian V. P. Franklin's review in the *Journal of American History,* for example, criticized Lewis's compulsive emphasis on detailing Du Bois's "sexual conquests. Du Bois devotees reading passages describing encounters projected as adulterous sexual liaisons are likely to respond as did the vast majority of Americans polled about the exposés associated with the Bill Clinton-Monica Lewinsky affair: these are private matters that may have occurred, but they are being shoved down our throats for political (or personal) reasons."

Franklin also questioned Lewis's stated goal of adherence to a "balanced" view of his subject, in light of the scathingly critical commentaries of Du Bois's work and writings throughout the first two-thirds of his book. "Although he does not employ the term, it becomes fairly clear that Lewis considered Du Bois a 'public intellectual' who functioned pretty much the same way as the contemporary crop of black pundits who believe their primary role is to explain the distinctive attitudes, beliefs, and practices of black people to white people," Franklin noted. This approach removed Du Bois from his proper political context. "Future generations of African-American scholars," Franklin explained, "must look to the example of Du Bois to understand the relationship between their research and writings and the improvement in the status of Africans in the world."

Historian Judith Stein voiced similar concerns about Lewis's second volume. "Lewis's sleuthing skills are superb and his breezy style and fine-tuned sensibility capture the social world of the Talented Tenth," Stein observed, "but these qualities do not equip him to probe in depth the politics that displaced its most talented member, the unstated theme of the biography." Lewis's second volume "soft pedals or ignores, but in the end does not analyze the politics that occupied so much of [Du Bois's] life." The central weakness, in Stein's judgment, was Lewis's inability or unwillingness "to find an underlying philosophy for the wide-ranging political choices Du Bois made throughout his public career."

From the moment Du Bois broke onto the national stage with the publication of *The Souls of Black Folk* and right up until the present day, he has been the subject of both scathing critique and sycophantic hagiography. His ideas have been silenced and subverted just as often as they have been championed and validated. After decades in which his legacy has been at the mercy of historians and politicians with covert agendas, let us return Du Bois, or at least our understanding of him, to the realm of revolutionary and radical politics—where he truly belongs. When we do so, we find overall coherence and purposefulness where others have encountered puzzling paradoxes and supposedly random behavior.

A "resurrection" of Du Bois-as-radical should start with a reconsideration of how he defined his intellectual tasks and public mission. Based on a full consideration of his entire career, I believe that Du Bois probably considered the tasks of the intellectual in much the same way as did literary scholar Edward Said. In his 1993 Reith Lectures for the British Broadcasting Corporation, Said advanced the notion that the "intellectual" should be defined as:

> an individual endowed with a faculty for representing, embodying, articulating a message, a view, an attitude, philosophy or opinion to, as well as for, a public. And this role has an edge to it, and cannot be played without a sense of being someone whose place it is publicly to raise embarrassing questions, to confront orthodoxy and dogma (rather than to produce them), to be someone who cannot easily be co-opted by governments or corporations, and whose *raison d'etre* is to represent those people and issues that are routinely forgotten or swept under the rug. The intellectual does so on the basis of universal principles: that all human beings are entitled to expect decent standards of behavior concerning freedom and justice from worldly powers or nations, and that deliberate

or inadvertent violations of these standards need to
be testified and fought against courageously.

Said's definition of the proper function and role of the intellectual within contemporary society presumes a radical
stance, an inherently critical posture located outside of the
mainstream. This is precisely how Du Bois throughout
most of his career envisioned his own purpose. This is not
to suggest, by any means, that Du Bois's political decisions
were always correct or even strictly consistent with his own
general political orientation. As progressive as he may have
been for his time on issues of gender, Du Bois was still a
product of the patriarchal and homophobic late Victorian
era. Du Bois did not, and perhaps could not, comprehend
that his patriarchal private life and progressive public life
could not be held in suspension from each other. The notion of a purely "public" intellectual is nonsensical. As brilliant and dedicated as he was, Du Bois did not model in his
personal life the changes he fought to achieve politically. A
social philosophy only becomes meaningful when it is
"lived" through the practical actions of human beings in
everyday life.

Despite these and other inconsistencies, Du Bois understood that effective scholarship had the potential to transform people's lives and could not be produced in isolation
from the daily struggles that largely defined their existence. By 1905, if not earlier, Du Bois was fully committed
to the construction of a social theory or social philosophy
of black liberation, which would be supplemented by the

empirical scientific investigations he continued as a sociologist and historian.

The first and most important element in the construction of Du Bois's social theory was a historically grounded critique of what scholars today describe as structural racism. Du Bois perceived racism, "the color-line," as a fully global phenomenon upheld by the politics of modern capitalism. The Jim Crow system in the United States was just a segment of that larger global system of racialized exploitation and empire. He recognized early on that structural racism on a global scale could not be overturned without a coordinated, mass democratic effort by people of African descent, Asians, and the other racialized minorities situated at Western capitalism's oppressed periphery.

Grasping this global perspective also helps to explain Du Bois's life-long fascination with Japan and India, two "colored" nations that had embarked on strikingly different paths to achieve parity and equality among the world's nations. The logic of Du Boisian antiracist theory and practice ultimately led to the Bandung Conference of 1955 and the birth of the nonaligned nations movement of the 1950s, most prominently represented by Nasser, Nehru, and Sukarno. Du Bois was not permitted by the U.S. government to attend the Bandung Conference, but he drafted a detailed memorandum for what he correctly believed would be a historic gathering. As historian Gerald Horne noted, "to the Bandung conferees, Du Bois was a vivid symbol of anti-imperialism and anti-colonialism and they openly showed their respect."

More than two decades ago Cedric Robinson suggested that Du Bois was the founding architect of a radical intellectual tradition that could be identified as "black Marxism." A review of the historical record, however, shows that an earlier generation of African-American radical intellectuals doubted that Du Bois possessed the political capacity to make the leap from the Talented Tenth to the struggles of the oppressed proletariat. In a short but remarkable and witty 1935 essay, "The Du Bois Program in the Present Crisis," sociologist E. Franklin Frazier dissected Du Bois's strengths and supposed contradictions as a left theorist. Frazier believed that "*The Souls of Black Folk* is a masterly portrayal of Du Bois's soul and not a real picture of the black masses." He contemptuously complained that "the voice of Du Bois is genuine only when he speaks as the representative of the Talented Tenth: for he is typical of the intellectuals who sprang from oppressed minorities." Du Bois's long-held attraction to socialism, in Frazier's judgment, was at best superficial:

> Since Du Bois is an intellectual who loves to play with ideas but shuns reality, whether it be in the form of black masses or revolution, he likes to display a familiarity with Marxian ideology. . . . In his *Black Reconstruction*, he played with Marxian terminology as a literary device. This is all as it should be, for Du Bois has said that there shall be no revolution and that economic justice and the abolition of poverty shall come through reason (the intellectual speaks), sacri-

fice (the romanticist speaks), and the intelligent use of the ballot (in the end he remains a liberal).

Frazier's judgments proved to be incorrect, as the social theory behind *Black Reconstruction* was ultimately revolutionary. Du Bois was attempting to chart the correlation between nontraditional reforms within a liberal democracy and the evolution of a new type of society.

The outbreak of World War II and the growing unrest in colonial Asia, Africa, and the Caribbean in the 1940s served to crystallize Du Bois's approach to Marxism. The best evidence of this is a series of extraordinary lectures and essays Du Bois produced during this period. In a remarkable lecture delivered at Vassar College in April 1942, "The Future of Africa in America," Du Bois insisted that "democracy cannot have a rebirth in the world unless it firmly establishes itself in America. It cannot establish itself in America if the majority of Negroes in the United States are disfranchised."

Du Bois extended the logic of his position to the Caribbean and Latin America as well, where antiracist struggles for political representation were also being waged under colonial and neocolonial regimes. The denial of full democratic rights for people of African descent in the Americas and the Caribbean was simply the "conspiracy of industrial exploitation, the rule of political oligarchies and the encouragement of future economic and race war." These are not the abstract musings or reflections of a "liberal." Rather, Du Bois was calling for wholesale changes—quite revolutionary at the time—in societies across the globe.

Shortly after his Vassar College lecture, Du Bois lectured at Yale University on "The Future of Europe in Africa," and he expanded upon similar themes. A general democratization of colonial Africa, which Du Bois was convinced would be the inevitable outcome of the current global conflict, would mean full, political self-determination. "The question as to what we want the future of African people to be; and what they themselves want, must be clearly envisaged," Du Bois argued. "Do we want them simply for their use to Europe, or do we look forward to a time when they are to be deliberately trained for their own usefulness to themselves and for their own development?" The successful democratization of colonial Asia and Africa, Du Bois was convinced, was the political prerequisite for a fuller and more comprehensive social transformation throughout the entire world. "As I look upon the world in revolution today," Du Bois concluded hopefully, "I can well believe that the Democracy which will crown the twentieth century will, in contrast to the nineteenth, involve the social control of the masses of men over the methods of producing goods and distributing wealth and services. And the freedom which this abolition of poverty will involve will be freedom of thought and not freedom for private profit-making."

Throughout much of his public life, and within his intellectual work, Du Bois crafted the black Marxism that resonated within the unique historical experiences and material interests of blacks and the American people in general. Another potentially fruitful way to approach the study of the radical Du Bois would be to place him within the larger tradition of what Perry Anderson has termed "Western Marxism." As in the writings of European Marxist intellectuals such as Jean-Paul Sartre, Georg Lukás, Herbert Marcuse, Walter Benjamin, and others, there is an overwhelming preoccupation with aesthetics and art in Du Bois. I once asked Herbert Aptheker to describe Du Bois in only one word, and he smiled: "Du Bois was an *artist!*" In the middle of establishing the NAACP and starting publication with the *Crisis,* for example, Du Bois was also writing his first novel, *The Quest of the Silver Fleece.* The Harlem Renaissance's explosion of "New Negro" literature a decade later prompted Du Bois to add his own expressive voice to the movement by writing *Dark Princess: A Romance* in 1928. Even during the bleak repressive years of McCarthyism and the Cold War, Du Bois's principal writings in the 1950s were his novels *The Ordeal of Mansart, Mansart Builds a School,* and *Worlds of Color.*

Like Jean-Paul Sartre, Du Bois also had a long pre-Marxist intellectual history prior to his political gravitation toward Marxism-Leninism. As a public intellectual, he repeatedly engaged in ideological contestation with the forces of reaction in an enormously wide variety of venues, from his regular newspaper columns in the African-American press to his two-year effort with novelist and lover Jessie Fauset in the 1920s to produce a lively children's magazine, the *Brownie's Book.*

In the early years of the NAACP, Du Bois wrote and staged the ambitious public pageant, "The Star of Ethiopia," which he described as "an attempt to put into dramatic form

for the benefit of large masses of people, a history of the Negro race." "The Star of Ethiopia" premiered in New York
City in 1913, marking the centennial of the Emancipation
Proclamation. The black pageant, with a cast of twelve hundred, was then staged in Washington, D.C., and Philadelphia
before World War I, and in Los Angeles in 1924. For Du
Bois and most other Western Marxist intellectuals, art was
inseparable from politics.

The inadequacies and incomplete character of Du Boisian
social theory, in the end, may have less to do with the shortcomings of Du Bois as an individual than with the objective
conditions and level of ideological and political development of the African-American people during the first half of
the twentieth century. Perry Anderson, paraphrasing Lenin's
famous thesis that "correct revolutionary theory . . . as-
sumes final shape only in close connection with the practical
activity of a truly mass and truly revolutionary movement,"
has argued that "revolutionary theory can be undertaken
in relative isolation—Marx in the British Museum, Lenin in
war-bound Zurich: but it can only acquire a *correct* and *final* form when bound to the collective struggles of the
working class itself. Mere formal membership of a party organization, of the type familiar in recent history, does not
suffice to provide such a bond: a *close connection* with the
practical activity of the proletariat is necessary."

Until the Great Depression, the majority of Du Bois's
political engagements and ideological contestations were
largely fought within, and on behalf of, the aspiring Negro
middle class. The black petit bourgeoisie as a group overwhelmingly sought full and unencumbered equality and

access within America's flawed democratic institutions. Even during the radical 1960s, the masses of working-class and poor black Americans continued to believe that the achievement of full political equality would lead inevitably to economic parity and private ownership. The social context in which Du Bois had to construct his arguments never approximated the revolutionary preconditions suggested by Lenin. Du Bois could only go as far as history could permit him to go.

What remains unfinished, for our time, is the building of the theoretical work, drawing upon Du Bois's courageous example that can advance the pressing struggles for human dignity and liberation of people of African descent, who today live under twenty-first-century global apartheid. The best way to honor Du Bois is to examine the intellectual output of his *entire career*—not simply one portion, phase, or phrase of it. By resurrecting the radical orientation and political trajectory of Du Bois, the true relevancy of his life, sacrifices, and struggles becomes clear. The final chapter of that magnificent legacy, the quest to achieve racial justice and genuine democracy, remains ours to be written.

Malcolm X's Life-After-Death

The Dispossession of a Legacy

Man, if you think Brother Malcolm is dead,
You are out of your cotton-pickin' head,
Just get up off your slumbering bed,
And watch his fighting spirit spread.
Every shut eye ain't sleep
Every goodbye ain't gone.
　　　　　—LEWIS MICHEAUX, PROPRIETOR,
　　　　　NATIONAL AFRICAN MEMORIAL
　　　　　BOOKSTORE, HARLEM

IN LATE APRIL 2005, THE UNCOMPROMISING IMAGE OF Malcolm X began appearing spontaneously throughout the Williamsburg section of Brooklyn. It was embossed on scores of buildings and dozens of garage doors, looking up from cracked sidewalks, and inhabiting the neighborhood subway stations. Etched beneath each stenciled portrait of the African-American militant were two words: "FORGET SELF." Many local residents, especially the white-collar (and mostly white) professionals who had recently relocated to the rapidly gentrified neighborhood, were puzzled by the fiery logo. But to the remaining members of Williamsburg's (mostly Latino, migrant, and black) working class, and to the small Muslim enclaves, no explanation of the image or the expression was likely necessary.

The local mom-and-pop businesses were being replaced with chain stores, and well-to-do apartments and townhouses were replacing the once affordable homes of those very same moms and pops. Resistance to the spread of this unchecked gentrification required a spirit of defiance, a determination to preserve the historical character of the neighborhood even if it meant ruffling the feathers of the privileged few. No single personality embodied that fighting spirit better than Malcolm X.

Several weeks after Malcolm X's reappearance in Brooklyn, on what would have been his eightieth birthday—May 19, 2005—the Shabazz family, city officials, and Columbia University representatives inaugurated the Malcolm X and Dr. Betty Shabazz Memorial Center. The new Memorial Center—featuring a life-sized statue of the black leader, a massive 65-foot-wide mural of scenes depicting his career, and six multimedia display kiosks featuring interviews with Malcolm X's associates and scholars—is located at the renovated remnants of the fabled Audubon Ballroom, the site of Malcolm X's February 21, 1965 assassination.

The Shabazz family explained that "the site of our father's tragic assassination has been transformed into an oasis of support for the principles he lived to achieve: peace, justice and equality for all humankind." The center's objective was "to promote a global understanding of the universal battle against all forms of discrimination." Lee Bollinger, Columbia's president, proclaimed at the center's opening that "this memorial represents an important chapter in our nation's history and is a significant achievement both for the Shabazz family and for Columbia University." A second, much larger public exhibit of Malcolm X memorabilia was simultaneously opened at the nearby Schomburg Center for Research in Black Culture of the New York Public Library. The Schomburg Center's director, Howard Dodson, proudly announced that his library's archival exhibit would infuse "new levels of interest and new levels of scholarship" into the life and times of Malcolm X. He went on to say, "We've consciously tried to stay away from putting a heavy interpretive line on it and to let Malcolm X speak for himself."

The Schomburg Center's exhibit features an impressive number of archival documents from Malcolm's childhood and youth. Included are an eighth-grade notebook in which classmates had penned their impressions of the teenager—such as "tall, dark, handsome" and "as a boxer fooey, as a friend, swell"—and letters from 1941 when the 16-year-old Malcolm was employed as a railroad waiter. The majority of items consists of family photographs; photos of Malcolm with other prominent black leaders of the 1950s and 1960s, such as Congressman Adam Clayton Powell Jr.; Malcolm's detailed, handwritten journals from his *hajj* to Mecca, Saudi Arabia, and his travels throughout the Middle East and Africa during 1964; and heavily annotated copies of his Bible and holy Qu'ran.

For serious researchers and scholars of Malcolm X, however, the exhibit left much to be desired. Reviewer Edward Rothstein of *The New York Times* noted that important documents pertaining to Malcolm X's public career were only "lightly sampled in this first pubic showing at the Schomburg Center. . . . Despite the new personal documents, there is something familiar about this exhibition, which does not offer new interpretations and misses an opportunity to delve more deeply into the difficulties of Malcolm's quest."

Curiously, major phases of Malcolm X's public career were minimally treated or completely ignored. Wallace D. Fard, the founder of the Nation of Islam in the early 1930s, is not depicted at all. Similarly, the powerful black nationalist influence of patriarch Elijah Muhammad, the Nation of Islam leader to whom Malcolm had dedicated his life and service throughout much of his career, is barely addressed. Rothstein observed that there was "also not enough explanation of the quarrel with Elijah Muhammad. . . . This exhibition . . . makes suggestions but seems reluctant to draw too many distinctions." No one even asked the most obvious question: Why had it taken four decades for the memorabilia of one of black America's most illustrious giants to be archived and placed on public display?

In spite of any perceived shortcomings, the Malcolm X and Dr. Betty Shabazz Memorial Center's formal opening was cause for celebration by Columbia's administrators, because it closed the book on a painful and costly decades-long struggle over the gentrification of the section of Washington Heights that had included the Audubon Ballroom building. I had been extensively involved since 1999 in lobbying the university to provide financial assistance and logistical support to the Shabazz family to facilitate the opening of this memorial facility. For years, Columbia administrators were implacably opposed to any involvement or material responsibility for making the assassination site accessible to the public. I had met with attorneys, city officials from New York's Economic Development Corporation, the city's deputy mayor, Schomburg Center employees, and Columbia's administration to broker an agreement. Even so, a deal was not brokered. It took five years, until December 2004, to open Malcolm X's assassination site.

Nearly a century ago, in 1912, Fox Theatrical Enterprises commissioned architect Thomas Lamb to design a public entertainment center. Lamb's finished building, the Audubon, located on Broadway between West 165th and 166th streets, featured beautiful terra cotta ornamentation. In the 1940s, when many of New York City's largest dance halls refused to accommodate black and Puerto Rican patrons, the Audubon became a major center for minorities. In the 1960s, Malcolm X and other African-American activists in Harlem rented the facility for public meetings and major events. In the 1970s, the City of New York acquired the property, which had fallen into disrepair. In 1982, Columbia University quietly proposed to the city government that it wanted to build a "space-age medical research center on the site, a biotechnology facility that would include a mix of University and private research facilities," and in February 1983, Columbia and the City of New York announced that they had reached an agreement about the sale and destruction of the Audubon.

Within days, black nationalists and Harlem residents devoted to the memory of Malcolm X were outraged that Columbia University was planning to tear down the site of his assassination. Some linked the refusal or inability of nearby Columbia Presbyterian Hospital to dispatch an ambulance literally across Broadway to attend to Malcolm X on February 21, 1965 with this latest maneuver by the city's third-largest real estate owner. AFRAM News Service declared, "Now, Columbia is purchasing Malcolm's tomb!" As opposition mounted, Columbia pushed back its timetable, with ground-breaking set for 1990. The new investment—$18 million of which was being provided by the cash-strapped city government—promised to stir economic revitalization in northern Manhattan, which by the late 1980s was in desperate economic shape. In the upper Manhattan area that extends from 155th Street to the island's extreme northern tip, there was one physician per 3,500 residents. Twenty-nine percent of all families in the district lived below the poverty level. The crack epidemic had ravaged the neighborhood and hundreds of strung-out homeless people routinely gathered in the massive 168th Street subway station. Columbia's new Audubon development promised a minimum of 275 jobs, with at least 65 "for neighborhood residents as maintenance crews, parking attendants, and office and retail clerks." In desperate times, the destruction of one physical site linked to one of black history's tragic events seemed a small price to pay for enhancing the commercial viability of the community.

Activists who mobilized residents to oppose Columbia's destruction of the Audubon noted that, according to a suppressed Environmental Impact Statement, 90 percent of all new jobs would go to Ph.D.s and professionals. In late 1989, a *Village Voice* reporter, Peggy Dye, observed: "The Audubon is on its way to effectively belonging to Columbia, one of the richest universities around. In a city where the poor cannot afford to take care of their health, where hospitals have closed and those that remain open labor with patient gurneys often crammed in hallways . . . the working poor, through the government, will subsidize a new frontier adventure for profit-making biology research, whose medicines they cannot afford."

In February 1990, approximately four hundred community activists launched the Malcolm X Save the Audubon Coalition (STAC) to halt Columbia University's development plans. Local organizers pointed out that the proposed demolition of the original Audubon was only the first phase of a projected $250 million reconstruction of northern Manhattan, which would quickly hike local housing costs, increase retail prices, and create relatively few employment opportunities.

Throughout the spring of 1990 hundreds of Columbia students participated in STAC's picket lines and protest demonstrations at the Audubon. STAC drove sound trucks through Harlem, placed tables on 125th Street in the central business district, and crashed public hearings, in coordinated efforts to squash the city's deal. In late 1989, with the election of David Dinkins, New York City's first African-American mayor, some critics of Columbia's expansion anticipated that the new administration would be sympathetic to the protesters. They were wrong: Dinkins was absolutely convinced that his political future depended on economic development and business investment in the city. Dinkins refused to seriously negotiate with STAC or with critics from the Society for the Preservation of Architecture. STAC in principle rejected the massive public subsidy that was required to fund Columbia's new building and demanded the full restoration of the Audubon as a multicultural resource and education center under direct community control. Scores of protesters were arrested, and several Columbia students who were actively involved in the demonstrations were disciplined and even expelled. Privately, Columbia President Michael Sovern was so frustrated by the public criticism and scrutiny of the university's business affairs that he seriously contemplated abandoning the entire project.

Finally in August 1990, the Dinkins administration concluded a "compromise agreement" involving the city government, Columbia, and Malcolm's widow, Dr. Betty Shabazz, who was at that time an academic administrator at Brooklyn's Medgar Evers College of the City University of New York. About 45 percent of the original Audubon Ballroom—including the actual physical site of Malcolm's death—would be saved, and an appropriate "memorial to Malcolm X" would be constructed inside the building, which would remain controlled by the city. The famed terra cotta façade of the historic Audubon would be preserved while the remaining superstructure—the ultramodern biotech facility—would be controlled by Columbia.

Columbia promised Dr. Shabazz that it would establish "Malcolm X scholarships" for minorities enrolled in its medical school. The deal didn't silence the critics, but it effectively ended popular resistance to Columbia's gentrification plans.

In October 1995, the newly renovated, reconstructed Audubon building was opened with great fanfare, under the new, Republican city administration of Rudolph Giuliani. Under the Dinkins administration, provisions had been made to subsidize the Malcolm X Memorial Center with rent payments provided by the Chase Manhattan Bank branch that occupied part of the first floor. Under Giuliani, however, that part of the agreement stalled.

Only several days before the tragic fire that would take her life, Dr. Betty Shabazz, accompanied by her grandson, Malcolm, met with Manhattan Borough President Ruth Messinger to complain about the lack of funding from the Giuliani administration. Dr. Shabazz's terrible death in 1997 briefly sparked a redetermination to finally open the Malcolm X Memorial. But within several months, interest in preserving the site died yet again. It was only in 1999, when Malcolm X's third oldest daughter, Ilyasah Shabazz, came directly to me with a personal appeal for assistance, that I became actively involved in seeking solutions to the impasse.

On May 19, 2005, with the formal opening of the Malcolm X and Dr. Betty Shabazz Memorial Center in the reconstructed Audubon, a phase of black history had come to an uncertain conclusion. Between 1990 and 2000, the percentage of Harlem households earning between $25,000 and $74,999 had jumped by 33 percent; about 8 percent of Harlem residents in 2000 earned above $75,000 annual income. Conversely, rents were rising at a steady pace, with 15 percent to 20 percent annual increases in the years following 9/11. Thousands of Harlemites whose families had lived three and four generations in the neighborhood were being displaced by black and white upper-middle-class professionals. Familiar neighborhood restaurants began to disappear, replaced by Starbucks, sushi bars, and banks. Tensions mounted between Harlem's business owners, real estate speculators, and political elites, who generally favored gentrification, and the shrinking majority of Harlem's traditional working-class and impoverished families who were threatened with displacement and eviction by the neighborhood's economic transformation.

Leith Mullings, in a 2005 article in *Annual Review in Anthropology*, suggests that structural racism's power is largely expressed through a predatory process of "dispossession through accumulation," a concept originally developed by geographer David Harvey. The wealthy upper classes are using their accumulated capital to profit at the expense of the working class and the poor, particularly racialized populations, by dispossessing these groups of things they either own or have acquired through collective struggle. This can include their land, their labor power, their right to vote, or their homes and personal property. Growing sectors of the black petit bourgeoisie now embrace policies of what Mary Pattillo describes as "black gentrification": the dispossession of urban properties occupied by low-income African Americans for the accumulation of profits for new black elites.

We may extend this idea of disposession through accumulation throughout the trajectory of black history. Forty years ago, both the U.S. state and the corporations hated and feared Malcolm X. For twenty years, the site of his physical demise rotted away, neglected and closed. There was absolutely no expression of interest, by the City of New York, Columbia University, the New York State Historical Society, or nearly anyone else other than working-class black people, to preserve all or part of that site for the purposes of posterity. It was only when Columbia's plan to develop a major bio-tech complex was approved and local African-American elites embraced their own strategy of black gentrification, displacing hundreds of low-income blacks from the Harlem neighborhood, that city officials moved to ensure the preservation and opening of part of Malcolm X's assassination site. Black historical preservation, they now recognized, was potentially profitable.

Corporate America can have a short memory, and it appears that in Malcolm X it no longer sees a feared symbol of change; rather it now sees the potential for dollar signs. The invitation for the gala opening of the Memorial Center had been sent to "VIPs" who were asked to "tailor your level of sponsorships." A minimal level of support required a donation of $350; at upper levels, "silver" supporters were expected to give $10,000, "gold" supporters $15,000, and "platinum" supporters $20,000. "We are offering our corporate friends an exciting opportunity to help us launch this important initiative," the Shabazz family's invitation letter proclaimed. Was this overture to "corporate friends" appropriate for the radical spirit and legacy of Malcolm X? After all, the deal that actually preserved the assassination site only occurred due to the tireless efforts of STAC and Columbia student protestors, yet neither former STAC activists nor antigentrification protestors were present at the new Memorial Center's grand opening.

The Shabazz family's interest in isolating Malcolm X from both his black nationalist phase and from his later connection with revolutionary socialism, along with Columbia's interest in burying the burden of its local history of public relations blunders and predatory behavior in Harlem, made an honest reckoning with the past impossible. Still, the greatest casualty in this process of accumulation by dispossession is Malcolm X, who is presently being "dispossessed" of the actual content of his words, ideas, and actual history. What has been preserved at the Audubon Memorial Center still remains largely an intellectually empty space, without meaningful political content or analysis. Malcolm's mesmerizing visage as displayed in a life-sized statue diverts us from pursuing hard questions about his relevance to contemporary struggles being waged about racism and power—questions that he himself would have asked. The contestation over the meaning of Malcolm X's life, and the cooptation of his historic legacy, began almost immediately after his assassination.

For many years, in the mainstream media and in grade-school textbooks, Malcolm X was most frequently juxtaposed with Martin Luther King Jr. These two central figures of mid-twentieth-century African-American political history were kept apart during their lifetimes by ideological conflicts and political rivalries largely beyond their control. In death, ironically, they continue to be pushed apart through selective quotations and image manipulation. To the masses of white America, Dr. King is favorably presented, preaching nonviolence and interracial harmony, whereas the militant Malcolm X advocates racial hatred and bloody confrontation. Even Malcolm's infamous slogan, "By Any Means Necessary!" evokes among many white Americans provocative images of Molotov cocktails and violent urban insurrection.

Despite these popular contrasts, both men strongly denounced black-on-black violence and drug use within the urban ghetto; both had vigorously opposed America's war in Vietnam and had embraced the global cause of human rights. In a 1989 "dialogue" between the eldest daughters of these two assassinated black heroes, Yolanda King and Attallah Shabazz, both women emphasized the fundamental common ground and grudging admiration the two men shared. Shabazz complained that "playwrights always make Martin so passive and Malcolm so aggressive that those men wouldn't have lasted a minute in the same room." King concurred, noting that in one play "my father was this wimp who carried a Bible everywhere he went, including to someone's house for dinner." King lamented, "That's not the kind of minister Daddy was! All these ridiculous clichés." Both agreed that these two giants were united in the pursuit of black freedom and equality.

As a child of the radical sixties, I was well ahead of the national learning curve on the King versus Malcolm dialectic. The chaotic events of 1968—the Vietnamese Tet offensive in February, President Johnson's surprise decision not to seek reelection, the assassinations of both Dr. King and Bobby Kennedy, the Paris student and worker uprising that summer, the police riot in Chicago at the Democratic National Convention—all affected me profoundly, creating within me a sense of political vertigo. By the end of that turbulent year, for the generation of African-American students at overwhelmingly white college campuses, Malcolm X rather than Dr. King became the symbol for the times we were living through. As the eighteen-year-old leader of my campus black student union, I reread *The Autobiography of Malcolm X* (New York: Grove Press, 1965) during the winter of 1969. The full relevance and revolutionary meaning of the man suddenly became crystal clear to me. In short, the former "King Man" (as I most assuredly had been) became almost overnight a confirmed and dedicated "X Man."

A number of Malcolm X's associates and others who had known him personally published articles and books in the late sixties, and firmly established the late leader as the true fountainhead of Black Power. For young black males, he personified everything we wanted to become: the embodiment of black masculinist authority and power, uncompromising bravery in the face of racial oppression, and the ebony standard for what the African-American liberation movement should be about. In actor Ossie Davis's memorable words, "Malcolm was our manhood! . . . And, in honoring him, we honor the best in ourselves. . . . And we will know him then for what he was and is, a Prince— our own black shining Prince!—who didn't hesitate to die, because he loved us so."

With Talmudic authority we quoted him in debates, citing chapter and verse, the precise passages from the *Autobiography* and books like *Malcolm X Speaks, By Any Means Necessary,* and other edited volumes. These collected works represented almost sacred texts of black identity. We even made feeble attempts to imitate Malcolm's speaking style. Everyone quoted him to justify their own narrow political, cultural, and even religious formulations and activities. His birthday, May 19, was widely celebrated as a national black holiday. Any criticisms, no matter how minor or mild, of Malcolm's stated beliefs or evolving political career were generally perceived as not merely heretical, but almost treasonous to the entire black race.

Working-class black people especially loved Brother Malcolm for what they perceived as his clear and uncomplicated style of language and his peerless ability to make every complex issue "plain." Indeed, one of Malcolm's favorite expressions from the podium was his admonition to other speakers to "Make it plain," a phrase embodying his unshakable conviction that the black masses themselves, "from the grassroots," would ultimately become the makers of their own revolutionary black history. Here again, inside impoverished black urban neighborhoods and especially in the bowels of America's prisons and jails, Malcolm's powerful message had an evocative appeal to young black males. *The Autobiography of Malcolm X,* the result of a collaboration between Malcolm X and Alex Haley, was released in November 1965 and sold six million copies internationally by 1977. By the late sixties, the *Autobiography* had been adopted in hundreds of college courses across the country.

Malcolm X's life story, as portrayed by the *Autobiography*, became our quintessential story about the ordeal of being black in America. Nearly every African American at the time was familiar with the story's basic outline. Born in the Midwest, young Malcolm Little became an orphan after his father was brutally murdered by the Ku Klux Klan, and his disturbed mother, overwhelmed by caring for seven little children, suffered a mental breakdown and had to be institutionalized. Malcolm relocated east to Roxbury and then to Harlem. There he became an urban outlaw, the notorious Detroit Red. Coming from a shattered home, this young African American had become a pimp, a hustler, a burglar, and a drug dealer. Eventually pinched by police, Detroit Red was sentenced to ten years of hard labor in prison, where he then joined the Black Muslims.

Once released, given the new name Malcolm X, he rapidly built the Black Muslims from an inconsequential black separatist sect to over one hundred thousand strong. But then Malcolm X grew intellectually and politically well beyond the Nation of Islam. He decided to launch his own black nationalist group, the Organization of Afro-American Unity, in 1964. He started preaching about human rights and "the ballot or the bullet." Malcolm made a pilgrimage to the holy city of Mecca, converted to orthodox Islam, and became El Hajj Malik El-Shabazz. He was acclaimed by

Islamic, African, and Arab leaders as a leading voice for racial justice. Then, at the pinnacle of his worldwide influence and power, Malcolm was brutally struck down by assassins' bullets at Harlem's Audubon Ballroom. This was the basic story nearly every activist in my generation knew by heart.

After Malcolm's assassination, his striking image and powerful rhetoric continued to resonate in various artistic expressions. Perhaps the most faithful commercialized representation of Malcolm X, at least from the standpoint of a culturally and politically authentic expression of the man's meaning to his people, was found in music and the arts. John Coltrane's "Afro-Blue," recorded soon after the assassination, may have been partially inspired by Malcolm. Far more influential in popularizing the Malcolm legend, however, was the black arts movement. Poets were particularly fascinated with the magnetic physical figure of Malcolm as a kind of revolutionary Black Adonis. In life, towering six feet, three inches tall and weighing in at a trim 175 to 180 pounds, broad-shouldered Malcolm X was mesmerizingly handsome, displaying a broad, boyish smile and was always spotlessly well-groomed. In photographs, he embodied strength and sensitivity. In death he would remain forever young.

Black women writers in the 1960s and 1970s frequently incorporated into their creative work the vibrant image of Malcolm X as a virile, masculine male, a model of what African-American manhood should be. Drawing from the images suggested by actor Ossie Davis's eloquent eulogy at Malcolm X's funeral, essayists and poets pondered the quintessential maleness of this charismatic man-child of black America. Celebrated African-American poet Gwendolyn Brooks captured these themes and images in her ode to Malcolm:

> . . . *He had the hawk-man's eyes.*
> *We gasped. We saw the maleness.*
> *The maleness raking out and making guttural the air*
> *and pushing us to walls . . .*

Sonia Sanchez, one of the most widely-read black nationalist poets of the period, was a Nation of Islam member for several years. Her Malcolm was less overtly the paragon of black masculinity than the tragic symbol of loss for what might have been, an unhealed wound that "floods the womb until I drown":

> *do not speak to me of martyrdom*
> *of men who die to be remembered*
> *on some parish day.*
> *I don't believe in dying*
> *though I too shall die*
> *and violets like castanets*
> *will echo me.*
> *yet this man*
> *this dreamer,*
> *thick-lipped with words*
> *will never speak again*
> *and in each winter*

when the cold air cracks
with frost, I'll breathe
his breath and mourn
my gun-filled nights.
he was the sun that tagged
the western sky and
melted tiger-scholars
while they searched for stripes.
He said, "fuck you white
man. we have been
curled too long. nothing
is sacred now, not your
white face nor any
land that separates
until some voices
squat with spasms."
do not speak to me of living.
life is obscene with crowds
of white on black.
death is my pulse.
what might have been
is not for him
or me
but what could have been
floods the womb until I drown.

Malcolm's powerful masculinity was most unambiguously on full display in Amiri Baraka's (LeRoi Jones's) famous and frequently-recited "A Poem for Black Hearts."

Despite its blatantly homophobic final passage, Baraka powerfully projected Malcolm X as the model for the perfect fulfillment of the black masculine ideal:

> *For Malcolm's eyes, when they broke*
> *the face of some dumb white man. For*
> *Malcolm's hands raised to bless us*
> *all black and strong in his image*
> *of ourselves, for Malcolm's words*
> *fire darts, the victor's tireless*
> *thrusts, words hung above the world*
> *change as it may, he said it, and*
> *for this he was killed, for saying,*
> *and feeling, and being*
> *change, all*
> *collected hot in his heart, For Malcolm's*
> *heart, raising us above our filthy cities,*
> *for his stride, and his beat, and his address*
> *to the grey monsters of the world, For Malcolm's*
> *pleas for your dignity, black men, for your life,*
> *black men, for the filling of your minds*
> *with righteousness, For all of him dead and*
> *gone and vanished from us, and all of him which*
> *clings to our speech black god of our time.*
> *For all of him, and all of yourself, look up,*
> *black man, quit stuttering and shuffling, look up,*
> *black man, quit whining and stooping, for all of him,*
> *for Great Malcolm a prince of the earth, let nothing*
> *in us rest*
> *until we avenge ourselves for his death, stupid animals*

*that killed him, let us never breathe a pure breath if
we fail, and white men call us faggots till the end of
the earth.*

While Malcolm X's overt influence receded somewhat
during the late 1970s and early 1980s, it wouldn't be long
before he was back on the cultural scene. Most of the artists
and groups who comprised hip-hop music's "golden age"—
from 1987 to about 1993—employed Malcolm to express
their own militant political and artistic messages. On their
classic 1988 album, *It Takes a Nation of Millions to Hold
Us Back,* Public Enemy generously sampled from Malcolm's speeches. In "Bring the Noise" they took two different excerpts from a Malcolm X speech for the provocative
phrase, "Too Black, Too Strong." Public Enemy's massive
popularity and its strong identification with Malcolm's image led other hip-hop artists to incorporate Malcolm X into
their own music.

In *Making Malcolm: The Myth and Meaning of Malcolm X,* cultural studies scholar Michael Eric Dyson correctly attributed Malcolm X's continued attraction as a
uniquely "black" cultural icon to "the characteristic quest
in black America," the search for a secure and empowering
black male figure. As "gangsta rap" emerged from the
West Coast and soon acquired national commercial appeal, these artists painted Malcolm X in their own violent
cultural contexts, replete with misogyny and homophobic
violence. Ice Cube's 1992 *The Predator,* for example, sampled a Malcolm address over a beat on one cut; on another,
"Wicked," Ice Cube rapped: "People wanna know how

come I gotta gat and I'm looking out the window like Malcolm ready to bring that noise." Tupac Shakur, perhaps the greatest individual artist hip-hop culture has yet produced, strongly identified himself with Malcolm X throughout his career. On Tupac's classic 1996 *Don Killuminati: The 7 Day Theory* album he provocatively asked on the song "Blasphemy":

> Why you got these kids minds, thinking that they evil while the preacher being richer. You say honor God's people, should we cry when the Pope die, my request, we should cry if they cried when we buried Malcolm X. Mama tells me am I wrong, is God just another cop waiting to beat my ass if I don't go pop?

Much of the hip-hop generation made the common mistake of juxtaposing Malcolm X versus Martin Luther King Jr., deploring the latter's commitment to nonviolence and the pursuit of meaningful reform within the system. Tupac Shakur, for example, questioned the limited information about Malcolm X in mainstream history texts and public school curricula in his debut album, *2Pacalypse Now*, released in 1991:

> No Malcolm X in my history text
> Why is that?
> Cause he tried to educate and liberate all blacks
> Why is Martin Luther King in my book each week?
> He told blacks, if they get smacked, turn the other cheek

Several hip-hop artists drew parallels between the narrative Malcolm X presented in his *Autobiography* and their own lives. The artist AZ the Visualiza, for example, on the 1995 album *Doe or Die*, identified himself with the "Detroit Red" gangster legend:

> My biography follows the footsteps of Malcolm X
> Money and sex, Gore-Tex Donna Karan and Guess
> Finesse, success through life
> Stress mics I blessed
> Puffing trees to get me high as trapeze

Some artists saw in the mature Malcolm's fearless political example the possibility of unifying a black community that was increasingly divided by class stratification and intragroup rivalries. Heavy D, in his 1991 album *Peaceful Journey*, declared optimistically:

> Malcolm X said, "By any means necessary."
> He didn't mean just for you, brother, he meant for
> everybody
> Maybe if we were still slaves, we'll be closer; however
> Pickin cotton was bad, but we picked it together

But other progressive hip-hop artists, aware of the terrible price Malcolm X paid for his political militancy, cautioned their audiences about the repressive power of the U.S. government in destroying black radical movements. One of hip-hop's most commercially successful singers,

Lauryn Hill, on the Fugees' 1996 album *The Score,* reminds her audience:

> If I lose control will send me to the penitentiary
> Such as Alcatraz, or shot up like al Hajj Malik Shabazz
> High class get bypassed while my ass gets harassed
> And the fuzz treat bruh's like they manhood never was,
> And if you too powerful, you get bugged like
>   Peter Tosh and Marley was.
> And my word does nothing against the feds

Malcolm X's words and persona were also incorporated into folk, rock, and popular music. In the 1988 song "Cult of Personality" by the group Living Colour, excerpts of Malcolm's voice emphasize the necessity to challenge oppressive institutions and to advocate thinking and living as free people. Popular white folk singer Ani DiFranco's 1999 song "To the Teeth" draws upon Malcolm X's controversial comments following the 1963 assassination of John F. Kennedy as a means to illustrate the continuing burden of racial and class injustices within contemporary America: "He said the chickens all come home to roost/Malcolm forecast the flood/are we really going to sleep through another century/while the rich profit off our blood?"

Hip-hop culture's expropriation of Malcolm as its "revolutionary muse" was one of two cultural sources that introduced Malcolm X to the black generation born after the Civil Rights and Black Power period. The other source was Spike Lee's 1992 biopic film *X.* Lee's film presented itself as a type of popular history designed for a large audience, but in virtually every respect it failed as any kind of credible account of Malcolm X's life. Presented in 201 minutes, the film related Malcolm's life as a three-act play: his Detroit Red hustler period in Harlem and Roxbury; his spiritual metamorphosis inside prison and emergence as Minister Malcolm X, leader of the Nation of Islam's Temple No. 7; and his final journey toward "true" Islam and a humanistic philosophy that informed his continuing commitment to black liberation. To Lee's credit, the film drew heavily upon the actual words of Malcolm X in numerous scenes—so much so that one critic in *The New York Times* complained that the film was "a tedious history lesson as opposed to dramatic entertainment." Following Alex Haley's lead, Lee minimized the federal government's fostering of disinformation between Malcolm X's Organization of Afro-American Unity and the Nation of Islam, which directly contributed to his assassination.

More disturbing, however, was the highly commercialized promotion of the film, which shamelessly turned the black leader's likeness into merchandise. As film studies scholar Thomas Doherty has noted, Malcolm X the movie was overshadowed by "Malcolm X the product." Hundreds of thousands of African Americans displayed portraits of Malcolm X in households and places of business. There were "X" posters, coffee mugs, potato chips, T-shirts, and caps. Even newly elected President Bill Clinton could be seen occasionally sporting his very own "X-cap" while jogging outside the White House in the morning. The *Philadelphia Tribune* estimated the commercial market for X-related products at $100 million in 1992. The "Malcolmania" hype had the effect of transporting the X-man from being merely a black superhero to the exalted status of mainstream American idol.

As with every mythic figure, the icon of Saint Malcolm accommodated a variety of parochial interpretations. To the bulk of the African-American middle class, the Malcolm legend was generally presented in terms of his intellectual and political maturation, culminating with his dramatic break from the Nation of Islam and eventual embrace of interracial harmony. For much of the hip-hop nation, in sharp contrast, the most attractive characteristics of Saint Malcolm were the incendiary and militant elements of his career. Many hip-hop artists made scant distinctions between Malcolm X and his former protégé and later bitter rival, Louis X (Farrakhan). Some would even insist that Malcolm X had never supported any coalitions with whites, despite his numerous 1964–1965 public statements to the contrary.

The hip-hop "Malcolmologists" seized Malcolm as the ultimate black cultural rebel, unblemished and uncomplicated by the pragmatic politics of partisan compromise, which was fully reflected in the public careers of other post-Malcolm black leaders, such as Jesse Jackson and Harold Washington. Despite their black nationalist cultural rhetoric, however, hip-hop Malcolmologists uncritically accepted the main parameters of the black leader's tragic life story as presented in *The Autobiography of Malcolm X*. They glorified Malcolm's early gangster career as the notorious, street-wise Detroit Red, and they tended to use selective quotations by the fallen leader that justified their use of weapons in challenging police brutality.

By the 1990s, Malcolm X had become one of the few historical figures to emerge from the black nationalist tradition to be fully accepted and integrated into the pantheon of civil rights legends, an elite of black forefathers that included Frederick Douglass, W. E. B. Du Bois, and Dr. Martin Luther King Jr. This privileged status was even confirmed officially by the U.S. government. On January 20, 1999, about 1,500 officials, celebrities, and guests crowded into Harlem's Apollo Theatre to mark the issuance by the U.S. Postal Service of the Malcolm X postage stamp. Few in the audience could ignore the rich irony of this event: One of America's sharpest and most unrelenting critics was now being praised and honored by the same government that had once carried out illegal harassment and surveillance against him. Ossie Davis may have captured the significance of this bittersweet moment better than anyone else when he jokingly quipped: "We in this community look upon this commemorative stamp finally as America's stamp of approval."

The Malcolm X postage stamp was the twenty-second in the Black Heritage Series, which had previously featured Frederick Douglass, Harriet Tubman, Martin Luther King Jr., Mary McLeod Bethune, and W. E. B. Du Bois. The U.S. Postal Service also released a short biographical statement with the stamp's issuance, noting that the retouched photographic image of Malcolm X had been taken by an Associated Press photographer at a Nation of Islam press conference held in New York City on May 21, 1964. The statement explains that soon after this photograph was taken, Malcolm X "broke away from the [Nation of

Islam]" and "disavowed his earlier separatist preaching."
The most generous thing one could say about this curious
statement was that it was the product of poor scholarship.
The photograph actually had been taken during an interview in Cairo, Egypt, on July 14, 1964. Malcolm X had
publicly broken from the Nation of Islam on March 8,
1964, two months earlier than the official statement suggested. More problematic was the U.S. Postal Service's assertion that Malcolm X had become, before his death, a
proponent of "a more integrationist solution to racial problems." But none of these errors of fact and slight distortions
disturbed most who had gathered to celebrate. The "Americanization" of Malcolm X appeared to be complete.

If Malcolm's Americanization culminated with the release
of a commemorative stamp in 1999, then the process arguably began in earnest with the publication of *The Autobiography of Malcolm X* in 1965. The individual most
responsible for removing the radical and revolutionary context from the image of Malcolm X was Alex Haley. Haley,
the celebrated author of *Roots* and coauthor of *The Autobiography of Malcolm X,* was a Republican throughout most
of his life and was a committed advocate of racial integration. He knew relatively little about the rich and complicated histories of both black nationalism and the various
religious organizations and sects affiliated with Islam that
had developed in the United States in the nineteenth and
twentieth centuries. He was not, unlike many other African-
American scholars who had studied the Nation of Islam's activities during the late 1950s, even mildly sympathetic with
the black group's aims and racial philosophy.

The Autobiography of Malcolm X was the product of an uneasy and at times contentious partnership between Malcolm X and Haley, who was a recently retired veteran from the Coast Guard and a feature stories writer. The two men were politically a continent apart from one another. To Haley, the separatist Nation of Islam was an object lesson in America's failure to achieve interracial justice and fairness. As Mike Wallace's controversial 1959 television series on the Black Muslims had proclaimed, they represented "the hate that hate produced." Haley completely concurred with Wallace's thesis. He, too, was convinced that the Nation of Islam was potentially a dangerous, racist cult, completely out of step with the lofty goals and integrationist aspirations of the civil rights movement. Haley was personally fascinated with Malcolm's charisma and angry rhetoric, but strongly disagreed with many of his ideas. Consequently, when Haley started work on the *Autobiography,* he held a very different set of objectives than those of Malcolm X.

By examining Haley's earlier journalistic writings, it is easy to discern his political bias and to anticipate his influence over the *Autobiography.* Haley's first published article on the Nation of Islam, "Mr. Muhammad Speaks," appeared in the March 1960 issue of *Reader's Digest.* While the article was a relatively accurate presentation of the Nation of Islam's activities and views, it was Haley's purpose to promote the arguments for integration to the *Reader's Digest*'s mostly white audience. "It is important for Christianity and democracy to help remove the Negroes' honest grievances and thus eliminate the appeal of such a potent, racist cult," Haley's article concluded.

Haley planned a follow-up piece on the Nation of Islam for the *Saturday Evening Post* in 1962, to be written with white writer Alfred Balk. The interracial team traveled throughout the country over a period of several months, interviewing Nation of Islam leaders and attending its public events. In early October 1962, Balk contacted the Federal Bureau of Investigation, explained that he and Haley were writing an article on the Nation of Islam, and requested the Bureau's "cooperation." On October 9, 1962, Balk was interviewed by an agent of the Bureau's Crime Research Section. Balk explained that his article with Haley, while providing "an accurate and realistic appraisal of the Nation of Islam," would emphasize "that many of the statements about the successes of the organization among the Negro people are also exaggerated."

The article that subsequently appeared in early 1963, entitled "Black Merchants of Hate," described the group as "a tightly knit Negro extremist sect." The article started with a detailed description of the dramatic events in Harlem on the evening of April 26, 1957, in which Nation of Islam member Johnson X Hinton was brutally beaten and jailed by New York City police officers. Johnson's beating drew hundreds of African Americans into the streets outside the 123rd Street police station in protest. This scene—now made famous by Spike Lee's film—illustrated the young Malcolm's tremendous authority and persuasive ability.

But the article also criticized other published reports that placed the Nation of Islam's membership between 100,000 and 250,000, and estimated its "hard core" base at only 5,500 to 6,000, with another "estimated 50,000 others who are sympathetic." At the conclusion, Haley and Balk cited a quotation from Little Rock, Arkansas, newspaper editor Harry Ashmore, which also expressed their own political views: "The Black Muslims are a warning to which churches, community leaders and public officials better pay heed . . . the masses of Negro people no longer are willing to stand still, that injustice has been done, and change is going to come. The only question is, will the change come through men and women working together regardless of race, or will the field be left to extremists?"

The significance of the Haley-Balk piece can hardly be overemphasized in providing the crucial template for the vast majority of subsequent commercially oriented and even scholarly interpretations of Malcolm X. First, both the FBI and the Nation of Islam were generally pleased with the article. The Nation had absolutely no problem being described as the black counterpart to white supremacist organizations. Being defined as a "black separatist sect" suited Elijah Muhammad's organizational objectives. Conversely, the Bureau was pleased with the willingness of Haley and Balk to recycle its internal surveillance information into their article. The memo stated that the article's objective was to "present the NOI to responsible citizens in its proper light which would enable the FBI to elicit cooperation from citizens and thereby carry out our [the FBI's] investigative responsibilities."

In outline form, many of the basic descriptive elements of Malcolm X's biography are contained in this brief article. Malcolm was described as a "lanky, energetic, good-looking man . . . once known in Harlem as 'Big Red.'"

Malcolm is presented as the son of "an uneducated Baptist preacher," a former numbers runner, "hustler of bootleg whiskey and dope," and an ex-convict. "Articulate, single-minded, the fire of bitterness still burning his soul, Malcolm X travels the country," the Haley–Balk article stated. "Many Muslims feel that Malcolm is too powerful to be denied the leadership [of the NOI] if he wants it." The FBI, Balk, and/or Haley were deliberately reinforcing the tensions within the Nation of Islam, by pushing the erroneous thesis that Malcolm desired leadership over the organization.

The *Autobiography*'s emphasis on Malcolm's pre–Nation of Islam years as a depraved criminal and notorious outlaw in Roxbury and Harlem, nearly beyond redemption, is without question an extreme exaggeration designed to illustrate the spiritual transformation he experienced when he submitted himself to the faith represented by Elijah Muhammad. The book was based on a series of taped conversations taking place over two years, and to some extent it reflects the compromises and contentious negotiations between its authors. The original manuscript, auctioned off by the Haley estate in 1992, shows extensive revisions and notations by Malcolm X in the organization and selection of details about his life.

Furthermore, although Haley grew to admire his subject, he remained deeply hostile to Malcolm X's black nationalist politics. Statements about Malcolm X made by Haley shortly after Malcolm's death seemed to me strangely negative. Haley asserted that both Malcolm X and Dr. Martin Luther King Jr. were going "downhill" before their deaths. Haley as a writer was primarily attracted to Malcolm's dramatic moments of epiphany—his conversion experiences first to the Nation of Islam, and then subsequently during his 1964 trip to Mecca. This emphasis helps to make the *Autobiography* an outstanding narrative that has continued to appeal to a universal audience. But its appeal for these very reasons—not unlike Frederick Douglass's autobiography—makes it less than reliable concerning important details about his life.

The basic approach agreed upon by the FBI and Balk in late 1962—to give a reasonably accurate depiction of the Nation of Islam but to represent the black separatist group as a product of American society's failure to implement liberal integration—remained Haley's consistent, overriding ideological objective in the *Autobiography*. Much important information that seemed to diverge from this central thesis was deleted from the narrative. For example, in July 1959, Malcolm X traveled extensively throughout the Middle East and Africa, even meeting Egyptian President Gamal Abdel Nasser and Deputy Prime Minister Anwar el Sadat in Cairo. He visited Saudi Arabia, Nigeria, the Sudan, Ghana, and quite possibly Syria and Iran. On July 26, 1959 at the St. Nicholas Arena in Harlem, Malcolm X informed his audience about his extensive travels throughout Africa and the Middle East, and even explained that he had tentatively planned to visit Mecca. The *hajj* to Mecca, he asserted, unfortunately had to be changed due to an illness with dysentery.

Yet the *Autobiography* barely mentions Malcolm's 1959 journey, giving this important excursion exactly one sentence. Lee's film deletes the 1959 trip from Malcolm's life.

Both the film and the *Autobiography* emphasize the central significance of his April-May 1964 travels as a spiritual-racial metamorphosis, a vivid illustration of the color-blind unity of humanity, which then becomes Malcolm's personal compass. This is playing fast and loose with history. Malcolm had been there and had seen nearly all of it before. In 1959, he returned from the Middle East still a committed, confirmed black nationalist and racial separatist. But in 1964, according to Haley's interpretation, Malcolm completely rejected the racism and extremism of his former self, largely due to his new "exposure" to peoples and cultures outside of the United States. A more accurate reconstruction of Malcolm's politics must place much greater emphasis on the continuity of his ideological and racial views as they were expressed throughout his public career, both while he was a member of the Nation of Islam and after he left that organization.

The so-called "miracle of Mecca," deliberately fostered by Malcolm X for the purpose of dramatizing his public break from the Nation's orthodoxy, was perhaps yet another construction, not unlike "Detroit Red" had been before. It also served Haley's interests to seize upon that new color-blind representation to underscore the thesis that black separatism constituted a dead end. Buried beneath all these deliberate reinterpretations was the hidden history of Malcolm's actual political activities, both inside and outside the United States.

A parallel process of constructing a public autobiography for the purposes of pragmatic politics might be found in Booker T. Washington's 1901 memoir, *Up from Slavery*.

Written with the assistance of journalist Max Thrasher, *Up from Slavery* introduced the Alabama educator to a global audience and provided the "Tuskegee machine" with a vivid, moving manifesto of individual accomplishment and personal sacrifice. It gave Washington access to corridors of power. Perhaps Malcolm viewed this partially fictive portrayal of his own journey up from prison in a similar light.

Looking through Haley's own papers and notes—which he had placed at the University of Tennessee's archives in January 1991—from the time of the writing would be the best way to decipher how much influence Haley really had over the *Autobiography*. Unfortunately, there remain unusual restrictions on scholarly access to his personal records. As luck would have it, several years before Haley's death, he had fortuitously named researcher Anne Romaine as his official biographer. Romaine was diligent and serious about her scholarly work. From the late 1980s until her premature death in 1995, Romaine had conducted audiotaped interviews with over fifty individuals, some of whom discussed Haley's role in producing the *Autobiography*. The great bulk of Romaine's papers and research materials pertaining to the *Autobiography* were also donated to the University of Tennessee's archives. Thankfully, there are no restrictions on Romaine's papers; everything can be photocopied and reproduced.

One folder in Romaine's papers includes the "raw materials" for chapter 16 of the *Autobiography*, which reveals the mechanics of the Haley–Malcolm X collaboration. Malcolm X apparently would speak to Haley in "freestyle"; it was then left to Haley to organize hundreds of sentences into paragraphs and then appropriate subject areas. Malcolm also had a habit of scribbling notes to himself as he spoke. Haley learned to pocket these sketchy notes and later reassemble them, integrating the conscious with subconscious reflections into a workable narrative. Although Malcolm X retained final approval of their hybrid text, he was not privy to Haley's editorial processes. Chapters the two men had prepared were sometimes split and restructured into other chapters. These details may appear mundane and insignificant. But considering that Malcolm's final "metamorphosis" took place from 1963 to 1965, the exact timing of when individual chapters were produced takes on enormous importance.

The Romaine papers also provide abundant evidence that any lack of coherence in the *Autobiography* was no accident. Something was indeed "missing" from the final version of the book as it appeared in print in late 1965. In his correspondence with Doubleday editor Kenneth McCormick, dated January 19, 1964, Haley described these chapters as having "the most impact material of the book, some of it rather lava-like." To find out what the contents of this "impact material" were, I contacted Detroit attorney Gregory Reed. In late 1992, Reed had purchased the original manuscripts of the *Autobiography* at the sale of the Haley Estate for $100,000. Reed has in his possession the three "missing chapters" of the autobiography which still have never been published. After several lengthy telephone conversations, Reed agreed to show me the missing chapters, which were kept in his office. With great enthusiasm, I flew to Detroit, and telephoned Reed at our agreed-upon time. Reed then curiously rejected meeting me at his law office, insisting instead that we meet at a downtown restaurant. I arrived at our meeting place on time, and a half-hour later Reed showed up, carrying a briefcase.

After exchanging a few pleasantries, Reed informed me that he had not brought the entire original manuscript with him. However, he would permit me to read, at the restaurant table, small selections from the manuscript. I was deeply disappointed, but readily accepted Reed's new terms. For roughly fifteen minutes, I quickly read parts from the elusive "missing chapters." That was enough time for me to ascertain without doubt that these text fragments had been dictated and written sometime between October 1963 and January 1964. This coincided with the final months of Malcolm's Nation of Islam membership. More critically, in these missing chapters Malcolm X proposed the construction of an unprecedented African-American united front of black political and civic organizations, including both the Nation of Islam and other civil rights groups. He perhaps envisioned something similar in style to Farrakhan's Million Man March of 1995. Apparently, Malcolm X was aggressively pushing beyond black fundamentalism into open dialogue and political collaboration with the civil rights community. Was this the prime reason that both the Nation of Islam and the FBI may have wanted to silence Malcolm X? Since Reed owns the physical property, but the Shabazz estate retains the intellectual property rights of its contents, we may never know.

Having seen the "missing chapters" I began to wonder what Malcolm X really had known about the final text that would become his ultimate "testament." Couldn't I discover a way to find out what was going on at Doubleday, which had paid a then-hefty $15,000 advance for the *Autobiography* in June 1963, only to cancel the book contract just three weeks following Malcolm X's killing? Doubleday's hasty decision would later cost the publisher millions of dollars.

The Library of Congress held the answers. Doubleday's corporate papers are now housed there. This collection includes the papers of Doubleday's then–executive editor, Kenneth McCormick, who had worked closely with Haley for several years during the writing of the *Autobiography*. As in the Romaine papers, here I found more evidence of Haley's sometimes weekly private commentary with McCormick about the laborious process of composing the book. These letters contained some crucial, unpublished intimate details about Malcolm's personal life. They also revealed how several attorneys retained by Doubleday closely monitored and vetted entire sections of the controversial text in 1964, demanding numerous name changes, the reworking and deletion of blocks of paragraphs, and so forth. In late 1963, Haley was particularly worried about what he viewed as Malcolm X's anti-Semitism. He therefore rewrote material to eliminate a number of negative statements about Jews in the book manuscript, with the explicit covert goal of "getting them past Malcolm X." Thus the censorship and repackaging of Malcolm X had begun well *prior* to his assassination.

On November 8, 1964, Haley contacted Doubleday executives, highlighting the significance of Malcolm's recent conversion to orthodox Islam, and the necessity "to quickly write a new last two chapters, which I am set to do, once I can get my hands on Malcolm." Haley gushed with enthusiasm: "Talk about a full-circle book. This will be it! From the toughest anti-white demagogue the land has ever produced to, now, 'All are brothers!'" Only days following Malcolm's murder, Doubleday editors decided to merge Haley's final two book chapters into one chapter; Haley in turn gave Doubleday "blanket permission to change any material you still deem libelous." This correspondence absolutely confirms that Malcolm X did not have the opportunity to read, review, or authorize the final text that bears his name.

The version of *The Autobiography of Malcolm X* that reached the public in late 1965 essentially represented three distinctly different books, produced for very different purposes by different people. Chapters 1 through 14, the core text of black nationalist orientation, depict Malcolm's fall into degradation, his prison experience, and his salvation by the Honorable Elijah Muhammad. These chapters were the product of Haley and Malcolm's collaboration between June and November 1963, prior to Malcolm X's silencing and subsequent break from the Nation of Islam.

The second book, chapters 15 through 19 (significantly shorter at 118 pages versus 270 pages) documents Malcolm's humanistic metamorphosis. Much of the text was written during the period when Malcolm X was out of the country, or only days before his death. During this time, Malcolm X was under constant death threats and was attempting to build a militant political group, the Organization of Afro-American Unity. He had, at best, a limited opportunity to review what would be widely taken for his political testament. The actual language at times clearly comes more from Haley than Malcolm X. Moreover, the three chapters that outlined a plan for creating a broad black united front under the Nation of Islam's aegis, working collaboratively even with blacks in the NAACP, the Congress of Racial Equality, and other integrationist groups, were completely deleted from the book. As a result, the *Autobiography* provides no clear political manifesto or agenda for black activism.

But even this degree of editorial control in Malcolm's "autobiography" was not enough for Haley. To make it absolutely clear that Malcolm had become, in effect, an integrationist, Haley inserted a third book, almost as long as the second, consisting of his lengthy "Epilogue" (pages 390–463) and an "Introduction" by *New York Times* reporter M. S. Handler, who had covered Malcolm X for his newspaper. In his introduction, Handler asserted that Malcolm had indeed experienced a "conversion to wide horizons." For Handler, Malcolm X was rapidly moving toward a "new approach, which in essence recognized the Negroes as an integral part of the American community—a far cry from Elijah Muhammad's doctrine of separation. . . . He no longer inveighed against the United States but against a segment of the United States represented by overt white supremacists in the South and covert white supremacists in the North." At the conclusion of his life, Handler added, "Malcolm sought to refashion the broken strands between the American Negroes and African culture." Nothing else is mentioned about Malcolm's political pan-Africanism, his growing attraction to socialism, or his demands for a United Nations investigation of human rights violations against black people inside the United States. Haley's personal accumulation—sales into the millions of copies of the *Autobiography*—would dispossess future African-American generations of much of the truly radical content of Malcolm X's ideas.

The Autobiography of Malcolm X has earned both Alex Haley and the Shabazz estate millions of dollars in royalties, and the book is widely recognized by scholars as a classic text in American literature. In 1998, *Time* magazine, ranking the most influential nonfiction works of the twentieth century, listed the *Autobiography* in the top ten. Malcolm X's rhetoric and dynamic use of language has been the subject of several hundred scholarly papers over the years. Yet apparently few scholars were prepared to address the difficult task of attempting to reconstruct the actual life of Malcolm X from his own primary sources.

By 2002, published works about Malcolm X had grown to roughly 930 books, 360 films and Internet educational resources, and 350 sound recordings. As I plowed through dozens, then hundreds of books and articles, I was dismayed to discover that almost none of the scholarly literature or books about him had relied on serious research which would include a complete archival investigation of Malcolm's letters, personal documents, wills, diaries, transcripts of speeches and sermons, criminal record, FBI files, and legal court proceedings. Some informative articles had appeared that were written by individuals who had either worked closely with Malcolm X or who described a specific event in which they had been brought into direct contact with the black leader. But these reminiscences lacked analytical rigor and critical insight. Nevertheless, the vast majority were all based on the same, limited collection of secondary sources and most largely accepted as fact the chronology of events and personal experiences as depicted in the *Autobiography*'s narrative.

Every historian worth her or his salt knows that "memoirs" like the *Autobiography* are inherently biased. All autobiographies are reconstructions of a person's life, drawn primarily from one's memory, which is always subjective, selective, and fragmentary. There are deliberate omissions, chronological re-ordering of events, and name changes.

Remarkably few books about Malcolm X, however, employed the traditional tools of historical investigation. Writers rarely conducted fresh interviews with Malcolm X's widow, Dr. Betty Shabazz, any of his closest coworkers, or the extended Little family. Writers made minimal efforts to investigate the actual criminal record of Malcolm X at the time of his 1946 incarceration. Not even the best previous scholarly studies of Malcolm X—a small group of books including Peter Goldman's *The Death and Life of Malcolm X* (1973), Karl Evanzz's *The Judas Factor: The Plot to Kill Malcolm X* (1992), and Louis DeCaro's *On The Side of My People: A Religious Life of Malcolm X* (1996)—had amassed a substantive database of documentation covering the subject's whole lifetime in order to form a true picture of Malcolm-X-the-man rather than the pristine icon. One constant problem in this was Malcolm X's inescapable identification as the quintessential model of black masculinity, which served as a kind of gendered barricade to any really objective appraisal of him or his legacy.

Texts of the actual transcripts of the majority of his speeches went unpublished for decades and many still remain unpublished. The major edited collections of Malcolm X's speeches, including *Malcolm X Speaks* and *By Any Means Necessary*, were published by Pathfinder Press and Merit Publications, which are affiliated with the Trotskyist Socialists Workers Party (SWP). The SWP, following the Marxist theories of Leon Trotsky, believed that the "revolutionary black nationalism" of militants like Malcolm X was a necessary precursor to the staging of a socialist revolution in the United States. The Trotskyists went out of their way to court and promote Malcolm X after his break from the Nation of Islam, and in many respects interpreted his ideals and goals as part of an "evolution" toward a revolutionary Marxist position. It is unclear whether the SWP intentionally edited Malcolm X's speeches to emphasize those particular views that conformed most favorably to their own dogmatic perspectives. What is indisputable, however, is that George Breitman, the Trotskyists' chief interpreter of Malcolm X, *never actually met Malcolm X himself,* and even the most famous and memorable speeches that Malcolm delivered, such as his "Message to the Grassroots" in Detroit on November 10, 1963, have only appeared in print in heavily edited versions, with major passages severely altered or completely deleted. The audio recording of "Message to the Grassroots" that was released on a sixteen-inch

record has many obvious sound gaps. Some of these omissions have been attributed to Malcolm X himself, who
asked for the deletion of all the favorable references to Elijah Muhammad that he made during the original address.
Consequently, millions of activists who read and quote
from the writings of Malcolm X are really unfamiliar with
what the man *actually said*.

Undoubtedly, the best "interpreter" of Malcolm X is
Malcolm X himself. However, the unwillingness or inability of the Shabazz family to make public his personal memorabilia and written manuscripts guarantees the continued
publication of confused, erroneous, and fragmentary literature about his life. By the mid-1990s, in the aftermath of
Spike Lee's film and the cultural explosion of Malcolma-
nia, a tremendous speculative market grew among private
collectors for letters, personal documents, or handwritten
notes by Malcolm.

One of the first indications of just how lucrative the
Malcolm X market could be was in March 1993, when the
carbon typescript of *The Autobiography of Malcolm X*
was offered for sale by Swann Galleries in Los Angeles.
The typescript, plus letters between Malcolm and Alex
Haley which were given a pre-sale value of $300–$400,
sold for nearly $6,000. In May 1999, the small, red per-
sonal diary that Malcolm X had on his body when he was
killed showed up in San Francisco. Butterfields, the nation's third largest auction house, was offering the diary
for a presale value of up to $50,000. The unidentified seller
had told Butterfields that he had purchased the 146-page
diary in the early 1990s from a sale of items from the New

York Police Department. Supposedly the diary, seized by police at the murder scene, had ended up being logged, stored, and subsequently stolen from a vault at the county clerk's office. Attorney Joseph Fleming, acting on behalf of the Shabazz Estate, was able to block the sale.

Inexplicably, however, the family failed to take corrective measures at this time to consolidate or inventory the remaining materials related to their father that were still in their direct possession. The theft and attempted auction of Malcolm X's diary triggered a new level of anxiety among one or more relatives in the Shabazz family. Sometime in early May 1999, a huge cache of invaluable items related to Malcolm X and Dr. Betty Shabazz was taken from the family home. Nearly all of these items had never been seen or appraised by scholars or archivists. Just a partial list of the items taken included: the private journals of Malcolm X's two trips to the Middle East and Africa in 1964; Malcolm's address book; his holy Qu'ran; outlines and texts of Malcolm's speeches, including the famous "Ballot or the Bullet" address he delivered on April 3, 1964, in Cleveland, Ohio; personal letters to his wife and brother Philbert; and a significant photographic collection and note cards.

On May 17, 1999, according to court records, the second youngest of Malcolm X's and Dr. Betty Shabazz's children, Malikah Shabazz Brown, signed a contract to rent space in a storage facility near Orlando, Florida. The materials transported from the family home were stored there for more than two years. The California-based owner of the Florida facility, Public Storage Inc. (PSI), later claimed that Malikah had failed to maintain the rent payments on the storage bin, and that the account was $600 in arrears. PSI determined that Shabazz Brown had defaulted on her contractual agreement, seized the locker's contents, and scheduled to put them up for sale on September 20, 2001. Technically, according to Florida law, a renter must receive a 15-day notice between the initial notification of a sale and the actual sale date of the items. However, Brown's first notice of the impending sale was dated September 7, 2001, only 13 days prior to the actual sale. As family attorney Joseph Fleming later observed, those two days should have made the sale null and void.

The Shabazz properties were purchased for the modest sum of $600 by a man named in court documents as James Calhoun. Calhoun reportedly offered the materials to Butterfields auction house, which agreed to do the public sale. An expensive-looking, colorful brochure was produced, highlighting the valuable features of the collection. Then in February 2002, Butterfields announced the pending sale of the Malcolm X collection, estimating its presale value at $300,000 to $500,000. When the Butterfields auction was announced to the public, there was a firestorm of criticism in the media, both in the United States and internationally.

Two public preview displays of the documents were scheduled in Los Angeles on March 8–10 and in San Francisco on March 15–17, with the sale to take place on March 20, 2002. At the Los Angeles preview display, Butterfields employees permitted potential buyers to handle the rare documents without gloves or other precautions. Observers were shocked to find many of the irreplaceable items severely yellowed and brittle—indicating that they had been stored haphazardly, and without any climate-controlled environment. The materials were subdivided and inventoried into twenty-one lots, and marketed at different price ranges on eBay.

What outraged historians particularly about the pending sale was the sloppy and inaccurate description of the items, indicating that no scholar familiar with the documents had been consulted and that no opportunity to assess their authenticity had been given. Most if not all of the immediate members of the Shabazz family, to my knowledge, had not been notified or even consulted in advance of the sale's announcement. In fact, I personally informed Ilyasah about the pending sale over the telephone. During a period of several frantic days, several major research universities and libraries independently approached Butterfields with the intention to purchase the entire block of items to maintain them in a single collection, which would then be preserved and made available to scholars and the general public. I happened to be in San Francisco when Butterfields made public its pending auction, and I held several conversations with its representatives. Butterfields demanded a generous commission of 17 percent of the sale price of the property, which pushed the total sale price to roughly $600,000. I had fully anticipated that several major research universities would be putting together bids.

My immediate response was to seek the Columbia administration's direct support to purchase the Malcolm X material. Provost Jonathan Cole offered his full support and authorization to bid on the property, with a commitment of $600,000, and more if that became necessary. But upon reflection, I wondered whether becoming an active participant in a bidding war was the most appropriate way to preserve Malcolm's legacy. Logically, the archives of Malcolm X should be located in New York City, and preferably housed in the community he knew and loved, Harlem. That would mean brokering a deal with the Schomburg Center and the New York Public Library, in partnership with Columbia. Provost Cole and James Neal, Columbia's libraries director, concurred with my assessment. Several days later I met Howard Dodson for breakfast at a Harlem restaurant that had been one of Malcolm's favorites. Dodson seemed to accept a tentative agreement of sorts. Columbia would finance the entire acquisition; the bulk of the property would be housed and displayed at the Schomburg; Columbia's Institute for Research in African-American Studies would digitize a subset of core research materials and correspondence and do much of the archiving and preservation.

Finally, on March 12, 2002, the pending sale came to an abrupt halt when PSI filed a suit in Los Angeles Superior Court, requesting legal clarification of the charges of irregularities involved in the acquisition and sale of the properties. Butterfields announced to the press that it had "received additional information from third parties that reveals a possible irregularity in the process of transfer of title, prompting the archive's removal from sale until the issue can be resolved. . . . In recognition of the exceptional scholarly and historical value of this collection, Butterfields has been engaged in extensive discussions with a number of public and private libraries, in the hope of negotiating a private party sale for the entire collection." Butterfields executives, stung by the nearly universal criticism of its business practices, clearly believed that their actions had been unfairly judged.

On narrow, but legally valid, grounds, attorney Fleming successfully regained control of the Malcolm X material from PSI and Butterfields. The Shabazz daughters decided to place the property on loan with the Schomburg and the New York Public Library. As the media attention died down, though, troubling questions still remained. Why had it taken the Shabazz estate nearly forty long years since the assassination of Malcolm X to begin the process of archiving and preserving his intellectual legacy? My initial impression was that the series of terribly traumatic events over the years—the firebombing of their home and Malcolm X's assassination in 1965, the bizarre arrest of Quibilah Shabazz for plotting the murder of Nation of Islam leader Louis Farrakhan in 1995, and the tragic death of Dr. Betty Shabazz in 1997 from injuries sustained in an apartment fire set by her grandson Malcolm—made it too difficult for Dr. Shabazz or her children to authorize the consolidation and archiving of Malcolm's intellectual agency.

Another possible explanation as to why the Shabazzes did so little to catalogue and preserve Malcolm X's papers came to light in June 2002, shortly after Butterfields's aborted auction. "Moments in Time," a company that sells rare manuscripts, famous signatures, and unusual memorabilia, advertised the availability for sale of a four-page, single-spaced letter, written by Malcolm X and addressed to Elijah Muhammad, dated March 25, 1959. The company made available a reproduction of the letter on the Internet, describing the document as "the most exceptional letter of Malcolm X ever to hit the market." The contents of the letter detailed the marital and sexual problems Malcolm X was experiencing with his wife of then one year, Betty. The letter stated that Malcolm X had been extremely reluctant to get married, and he vigorously denied widely whispered accusations that he had engaged in sexual relations with several female Nation of Islam members. "I stayed single for a long time because I knew my own weaknesses and shortcomings," Malcolm professed. He would later admit that, "when I did marry it was at a time of great mental and spiritual weakness on my part." The letter revealed that soon after marriage, the relationship quickly drifted "down hill." Malcolm complained to his mentor about his spouse's "luxurious tastes which I immediately began to curb." But the underlying tension between the couple, Malcolm admitted, was sexual. In frank and surprisingly explicit language, the letter described certain sexual intimacies and details about Betty's profound unhappiness and lack of fulfillment with Malcolm's lovemaking.

The international media of course immediately picked up the story and, predictably, put its own perverse spin on the provocative revelations. In the London *Independent,* journalist Sholto Byrnes speculated, "The letter is on sale for $125,000 . . . and I imagine Muhammad's advice on how to get things up at home would fetch a similar sum." The *New York Post* reported the sexual revelations under the bold headline, "Malcolm X's Sexual Suffering." The African-American leader, according to the *Post,* "was a henpecked husband who couldn't keep up with his wife's sexual demands."

Critics of the letter's release promptly protested that the intimate sexual details of Malcolm X and Dr. Shabazz were completely irrelevant to a historical appreciation of their lives. Nevertheless, important details about a historical figure's intimate personal relationships, and even sexual preferences, can be illuminating in revealing a full human portrait of that individual. For example, James Baldwin's well-known homosexuality was a central dimension of his personality, and key to understanding how he lived his life and defined his art and politics. Martin Luther King Jr.'s now widely reported, enormous sexual appetite for women may appear to add little to an understanding of his politics and the activities of his public life, but one must also acknowledge that the personal is always ultimately political. There are no absolute boundaries that separate the sexual needs and desires of individuals from the roles they attempt to play in public life, and in how they relate to other human beings in very intimate ways.

Therefore, any serious study of Malcolm X would be incomplete without a full examination of his complicated relationships with his wife and children, siblings and relatives, and closest associates. There is much that is already known, for example, about the difficulties within Malcolm X's marriage with Betty Shabazz. In the *Autobiography,* Malcolm X openly revealed deeply misogynistic, patriarchal views about women in general, and serious misgivings about his wife. When he first was released from prison and became a Muslim minister, Malcolm X was firmly convinced that "a woman's true nature is to be weak," and that any man "must control [his woman] if he expects to get her respect." During one interview with Haley, Malcolm X observed that "you never can fully trust any woman . . . I've got the only one I ever met whom I would trust seventy-five percent. I've told her that. . . . I've seen too many men destroyed by their wives, or their women."

The "Moments in Time" letter makes clear that Malcolm X did not want to get married, but the social expectations of his role as a minister pressured him into hasty matrimony. Malcolm X researcher Karl Evanzz has suggested that Malcolm X had, prior to his marriage to Betty X, been attracted to another woman in Temple No. 7, Evelyn X. Supposedly, when Evelyn X was informed about Malcolm's unexpected marriage to Betty Shabazz, she left the temple in tears. Elijah Muhammad then became sexually involved with her. As Evelyn X Williams later informed the press in 1964, "[Elijah Muhammad] told us that under the teaching of the Holy Koran, we were not committing adultery and that we were his wives." In my subsequent oral history interview with Louis Farrakhan, he confirmed that Malcolm's deep attraction for Evelyn continued throughout his marriage, and that he even seriously considered relocating her from Chicago back to his Mosque No. 7 in the early 1960s, prior to his rupture from Muhammad. Louis X (Farrakhan) had to sternly persuade his mentor not to take this action, reminding Malcolm that "he was a married man!"

Malcolm should not have been completely surprised by the sexual relationship culminating in pregnancies that developed between Muhammad and Evelyn X. Indeed, he later admitted in the *Autobiography* that "as far back as 1955, I had heard hints" about Muhammad's serial adultery. But the deep ambivalence he felt concerning marriage in general, and the problems that Betty had with his controlling and patriarchal behavior, probably did not sustain a strong, trusting relationship between the two. This is possibly the reason that, when Malcolm broke from the Nation of Islam and created the Organization of Afro-American Unity in 1964, he strictly limited Betty's attendance and involvement inside the new group.

Malcolm X's relationships with many of his family members were even more problematic. Most of Malcolm X's siblings—Wilfred, Philbert, Reginald, and Hilda—had joined the Nation of Islam in the 1940s, prior to his own conversion while in prison. Malcolm unquestionably accepted the edicts and restrictions membership in the Nation of Islam required, even to the point of ostracizing a family member who did not live up to these extremist standards. When Malcolm X's younger brother Reginald was disciplined and placed on suspension by Elijah Muhammad for having a sexual affair with the secretary of the New York Temple, Malcolm X coldly rejected him.

Years later, when Malcolm X was first "silenced" and then forced out of the Nation of Islam, Wilfred and Philbert remained blindly loyal to Elijah Muhammad and the Chicago headquarters. Indeed, only days following Malcolm X's assassination, Wilfred X, the minister of Detroit's mosque, and Philbert X, the head of Lansing's mosque, lavishly praised the leadership of Muhammad and denounced their late brother before thousands at the Nation of Islam's annual "Savior's Day" convention in Chicago. Philbert X harshly condemned his brother for "traveling on a very reckless and dangerous road." Pointing then to Elijah Muhammad, Philbert X poignantly added, "Where he leads, I will follow." Tracking these complicated sets of relationships between the members of the extended Little family through oral interviews should provide new insights, restoring Malcolm's own voice to the cacophony of well-meaning but ridiculously erroneous interpretations about who he really was.

At Malcolm X's Harlem funeral in 1965, celebrated actor/ activist Ossie Davis's eulogy and memorable description of Malcolm X as a "black shining prince" captured both the tragedy and triumph of the moment. Interviewing my friend Ossie during the summer of 2003, I asked why he had used that particular word: "prince." Ossie replied that Malcolm X had inspired awe and admiration among black people worldwide, and deep love among the residents of Harlem in particular, because he consistently spoke truth to power. "He was the person that we wished we all could be." But blended throughout the fabric of myth and legend was also tremendous pain and sadness. "A prince," Ossie explained, "is not a king." Malcolm's greatness is found in his personal determination to become much more than he was. His life's complex journey had been brutally cut short, his potential unfulfilled.

C. L. R. James made a similar observation about Malcolm X in a 1967 London lecture. James described him as "that great fighter whose potentialities were growing so fast that his opponents had to get rid of him." James certainly did not share Malcolm's rapidly evolving black nationalist political philosophy, but it is not difficult to imagine "Nello" interrogating the militant black Muslim in an intense but casually intimate, lengthy conversion. After all, Nello had an enormous curiosity about peoples and cultures of all kinds, and he particularly wanted to identify and to comprehend the historical and social forces that constructed and produced such a remarkable personality as Malcolm X.

Yet the Americanization and commodification of El Hajj Malik El Shabazz is now well underway. For all of the reasons I've outlined—including Haley's ideological manipulations to transform the black nationalist militant into a liberal integrationist, the suppression of Malcolm X's memorabilia by private collectors, and his family's subsequent attempts to keep the man and his legacy from public scrutiny—the real voice and vision of Malcolm X has been, and is presently being, dispossessed from the intellectual and cultural memory of black America. We must never forget that the *real* Malcolm X was infinitely more remarkable than the personality presented in the *Autobiography,* in Spike Lee's film, or in Tupac's rhymes.

The man who was born in Omaha, Nebraska, as Malcolm Little, and who perished in the Audubon Ballroom as El Hajj Malik El Shabazz, was no saint. He made many

serious errors of judgment, several of which directly contributed to his murder. Yet despite these serious contradictions and personal failings, Malcolm X also possessed the
unique potential for uniting black America in an unprecedented coalition with African, Asian, and Caribbean nations. He alone could have established unity between Negro
integrationists and black nationalists inside the United
States. He possessed the personal charisma, the rhetorical
genius, and the moral courage to inspire and motivate millions of blacks into unified action. Neither the *Autobiography* nor Spike Lee's 1992 movie revealed this powerful
legacy of the man, or explained what he could have accomplished. What continues to be suppressed and censored in
Malcolm's past also tells us something about the dispossession of black heritage from black people themselves, which
exists even to this day.

Malcolm X was potentially a new type of world leader,
personally drawn up from the "wretched of the earth," who
could have moved into the political stratosphere of international power. Haley's integrationist interpretation of Malcolm X's career nearly dispossessed the black leader from
pan-Africanist militancy and black internationalism. Today,
celebrated hip-hop artists such as 50 Cent promote for personal profit another kind of gangsta rap dispossession:

> I'm like Paulie in Goodfellas, you can call me the Don
> Like Malcolm by any means, with my gun in my palm
> Slim switched sides on me, let niggas ride on me
> I thought we was cool, why you want me to die homie?

Only by preserving and making available to the public the actual contents of Malcolm X's writings and speeches can people of African descent, as well as other oppressed people, reclaim his authentic legacy in order to transform their futures.

The Unfulfilled Promise of *Brown*

From Desegregation to Global Racial Justice

Until the philosophy which holds one race
Superior and another inferior
Is finally and permanently discredited and abandoned
Everywhere is war, me say war
That until there is no longer first class
And second class citizens of any nation
Until the colour of a man's skin
Is of no more significance than the colour
of his eyes
Me say war . . .
        —BOB MARLEY, "WAR"

IT WAS SUNNY AND WARM ON AN EARLY FRIDAY afternoon in mid-September 2004, the kind of brilliant moment one yearns for in the bleakness of a New York City winter. Classes at Columbia University had just started up again, and hundreds of students were clustered along

the steps of Low Library, sunbathing and leisurely enjoy-
ing their company and their conversations. I hurriedly
navigated my way down the steps of this human obstacle
course, embarrassed at being uncharacteristically late for
a lunch appointment. Finally, walking quickly down the
thoroughfare of Columbia's mall, I could see the law school
at the corner of Amsterdam Avenue and West 116th Street.
Crossing against the light, I searched the crowd frantically
for my guest. Cool as a cucumber, legendary eighty-seven-
year-old Federal Judge Robert L. Carter was already there,
patiently waiting for me to arrive. "Not to worry," Judge
Carter smiled warmly, grasping my hand firmly. "It's a
lovely day."

It's not often that a historian has a lunch date with an
icon of African-American history. But lunch with Robert
Carter, former general counsel to the NAACP and the original attorney of the 1954 *Brown v. Board of Education* decision, was exactly that. Judge Carter is remarkably youthful
and vigorous in appearance, still physically trim, dapper in
dress, and his mental dexterity is as extraordinarily sharp as
it was in those legendary court battles a half century ago.

Yet for one who has accomplished so much in a celebrated career of public service and social justice advocacy,
Carter's manner is remarkably modest. He casually explained
over lunch that his deep interest in African-American history, especially the experiences of struggle by blacks during
Reconstruction, had motivated him toward pursuing a law
degree at Howard University so many years ago. It was at
Howard on November 8, 1938, that Carter, still a student,
witnessed the incomparable civil rights attorney, Charles

Hamilton Houston, rehearse the arguments he would successfully employ before the Supreme Court the next day in what would be called the *Gaines* case.

Hamilton's victory in *Gaines* over the all-white law school of the University of Missouri would sow the seeds for some of Judge Carter's greatest moments and pave the road toward the ultimate triumph over all segregated education many years later. Today, Robert Carter is best known as one of the principal attorneys who won the famous *Brown v. Board of Education* case, which along with four other cases culminated in the U.S. Supreme Court's 1954 decision outlawing racial segregation in public schools. But the political story behind this remarkable civil rights achievement is too little appreciated.

Robert Lee Carter was born in Careyville, Florida, on March 11, 1917, one of nine children. Soon after Robert's birth, the Carter family migrated north, moving to New Jersey. Robert's father soon died, and the Carter family struggled to survive. Robert's mother worked for years as a laundress to support and educate her children. Robert attended high school in Newark, where his outstanding academic record earned him a college scholarship at all-black Lincoln University in Pennsylvania. Earning his BA degree from Lincoln University, Carter subsequently received his law degree at Howard. After receiving a Rosenwald Fellowship, Carter enrolled in graduate study at Columbia University.

After military service during World War II, Carter joined the NAACP Legal Defense and Education Fund (LDF), and quickly rose as second-in-command to the LDF's charismatic and capable leader, attorney Thurgood Marshall.

Over our lunch Judge Carter talked fondly about his early experiences on Marshall's staff back in the 1940s and 1950s. I reminded him that for a time the offices of Marshall and W. E. B. Du Bois were adjacent to each other, much to Du Bois' great displeasure. Carter laughed aloud, immediately recalling Marshall's habit of caucusing with his talented legal assistants at the end of a hard workday in boisterous, smoke-filled bull sessions around his office at late hours. The constant noise, and not infrequently ribald, earthy language, Carter tastefully explained, greatly irritated the proper African-American scholar. Carter's small office was right down the hall, so he had a ringside seat to the sometimes tense relationship between these two legends of black history. I sat listening to Carter in quiet admiration: He had not only witnessed the personal relationship between historical figures; he had also shaped the course of black history by the monumental decisions he had personally made.

In his autobiography, *A Matter of Law*, Carter revealed that as a young attorney he often worried that he "might never be a good or successful lawyer." He was not gifted with an oratorical speaking voice, and he "did not have the desire or personality to be a civil rights leader who could stir the masses to action." Because he had no burning passion to become a great leader of men, Carter decided that his proper role should be that of mastering civil rights–related law, becoming "thoroughly conversant with every factual detail involved and have at my fingertips every aspect of the law applicable to the case being presented." Early in his life Carter grasped the power of litigation to effect change either by formal court decree or by a verdict handed down by the larger, and more fickle, court of public opinion. In 1949, Carter and attorney Constance Baker Motley lost a case involving salary discrimination against black teachers in Jackson, Mississippi, but the continued pressure, both legal and otherwise, soon forced the state legislature to equalize teachers' salaries regardless of race. What was memorable to Carter about this case, however, was the emancipatory power that their presence in that courtroom gave to local African Americans:

> Blacks crowded the courtroom, and the trial became public theatre. They took vicarious pride in our performances in court and reenacted scenes from the trial in barbershops and beauty parlors, at parties, in backyards, wherever groups gathered. We provided hope that their exploitation, hurt, and humiliation because of being black might be eliminated someday. I also believe we instilled in some boys and girls the desire to study law.

One of the most striking, and groundbreaking, aspects of Carter's civil rights litigation was the close integration of antiracist scholarship in the development of legal initiatives designed to undermine Jim Crow segregation. In 1950, for instance, Marshall sponsored an academic advisory conference at Howard University to assist in the development of their brief in the *McLaurin v. Oklahoma State Regent* desegregation case. Prominent among the participating scholars, Carter now recalls, was Du Bois, who delivered a stunningly detailed critique of the economic exploitation of blacks under Jim Crow. With a characteristic flourish, Du Bois ended his lecture with the admonition, "Know the facts and the facts will set you free." Similarly, in the preparations for the reargument of *Brown v. Board of Education* before newly appointed Supreme Court Chief Justice Earl Warren in 1953, Carter and other LDF attorneys caucused with historians John Hope Franklin, Rayford Logan, C. Vann Woodward, and other scholars. Their role was to assist Carter, Marshall, and the other attorneys in reviewing the historical evidence that could be employed to challenge the legitimacy of Jim Crow segregation.

The most significant precedent that Carter and his colleagues had to reverse in their difficult struggle to bring down Jim Crow was *Plessy v. Ferguson*. In 1896, the Supreme Court had declared that racially segregated schools were constitutional, provided that all-black schools were "separate but equal" to white schools. In reality, however, the separate-but-equal standard created and perpetuated gross inequalities in African Americans' access to education, especially in the Jim Crow South. The NAACP's attorneys, first led by Houston, and subsequently by Marshall, launched a series of successful legal challenges against unequal access in education over a quarter century.

Though these early cases did not challenge the principle of "separate but equal" head on, they nevertheless did lay the foundation for a direct assault on the legality of Jim Crow education. It was not until 1950 that Marshall and NAACP leader Walter White were sufficiently confident that the legality of racial segregation could be successfully assaulted in education cases before the high court.

Carter—as Marshall's chief lieutenant—was central in mapping the entire legal strategy. It was Carter who contacted social scientists Kenneth and Mamie Clark, whose studies establishing the destructive psychological effects of racial exclusion on black children provided an important rationale for the legal argument to outlaw separate schools. Carter and his colleagues argued that the *Plessy* standard was unconstitutional because it denied equality under the law to Negroes as stipulated in the Fourteenth Amendment. But hedging their bets, just in case the Supreme Court refused to overturn the *Plessy* precedent, they also pointed out that even *Plessy* mandated fully "equal" educational facilities for Negroes. The only way to establish true equality was to integrate all public schools.

On May 17, 1954, in a surprisingly unanimous decision, the Supreme Court ruled in favor of the LDF, the NAACP, and the plaintiffs in *Brown* and the other cases. Supreme Court Chief Justice Earl Warren, in his decision, declared: "Does segregation of children in public schools solely on the basis of race, even though the physical facilities and other tangible factors may be equal, deprive children of the minority group of equal educational opportunities? We believe it does. . . . We conclude, unanimously, that in the field of public education, the doctrine of 'separate but equal' has no place. Separate educational facilities are inherently unequal." The *Brown* decision of 1954 set the legal framework for the emergence of the modern black freedom movement of the 1950s and 1960s. According to legal scholar Derrick Bell, the triumph of *Brown* "offered a much-needed reassurance to American blacks that the precepts of equality and freedom so heralded during World War II might yet be given meaning at home." The new movement would succeed in overturning legal racial segregation in all public accommodations and institutions a decade later with the passage of the 1964 Civil Rights Act.

Carter devoted his life to the civil rights crusade led by the NAACP, but he did not always agree with the organization's political orientations and internal policies. In *A Matter of Law,* Carter observes that Roy Wilkins by the 1960s had "become wedded to a belief that the NAACP's survival required it to ally itself to the fortunes and policies of liberal Democrats." This approach to the achievement of greater racial fairness would prove politically disastrous over time. "I opposed this alliance with the Democrats," Carter insists, "not only of the NAACP but of blacks in general . . . we give up whatever clout we might wield, and then Democrats take us for granted, and then propose policies adverse to us to lure white voters." Carter wisely anticipated the protracted struggles and years of political maneuvering that lay ahead. Still, the legal victories achieved by Carter, Marshall, Houston, and other brilliant African-American lawyers radically changed the way that "race" was "lived" in daily life for millions of blacks.

My own story, growing up in the American Midwest in Dayton, Ohio, was typical of many others in the post-*Brown* generation. I was able to enroll in an integrated elementary school in 1956, but I could never for a single instant, ever forget that I was black. Even in a Midwestern town where legally sanctioned segregation did not exist, the barrier of race isolated us from opportunities in thousands of ways. When my father attempted to obtain a mortgage—to purchase a house to start a nursery school business—he was denied credit at every single bank in metropolitan Dayton. At the time Negroes were confined largely to the city's west-side ghetto, and were usually not allowed to purchase homes or even to rent apartments in many quarters of the city. Growing up in the 1950s, I could vividly comprehend that as Negroes we lived in a separate, unequal world.

Yet within that segregated world, we found our own joys and rejoiced at the sound of our own laughter; we found a resilient music and relentless dignity within our souls. We prayed to the Lord in our own houses of worship, and celebrated our own heroes every February during "Negro History Week." The principles and policies of American democracy, the core values and ideals in which Negroes deeply believed, were never fully extended to us. When we sang our national anthem, it was James Weldon Johnson's "Lift Ev'ry Voice and Sing." Our tenuous status as permanent outsiders gave us a peculiar insight into the nature and unequal reality of white power.

Beyond the veil of race stood another bastion of unequal power and structural violence called poverty. I gradually learned to recognize the different manifestations of social inequality: the unemployed laborers who clustered along Fifth Street desperately seeking a day's wages, while affluent whites drove by, deciding which man would be hired; the factory workers living in our neighborhood who came home at dusk, filthy and tired; the middle-aged black women standing at the bus stop just before dawn, leaving their own children to travel across town to care for the children of well-to-do families in Kettering and Oakwood. Traveling to the South every August to attend the annual Marable family reunion in Tuskegee, I saw a chain gang when I was about eleven years old. I watched in silence as our family automobile slowly passed the work gang along the side of a country road just as we crossed the state boundary entering Alabama. The men—roughly chained together at their ankles—wore coarse garments that were striped white and black. White guards with guns, loaded, menacing, and glaring under the scorching sun, supervised their labor. It was a shocking scene I could never forget.

Although my education in the harsh realities of race in America had certainly begun for me at a very young age, I received my first real lessons in politics in the early 1960s, with the eruption of public protests during the Civil Rights movement, America's "second Reconstruction." On television, along with millions of other Americans, I witnessed a series of unprecedented, powerful confrontations: the sit-in movement, initiated in February 1960 by a group of college students in North Carolina and escalating to hundreds of nonviolent protests across the South; the Freedom Rides led by the Congress of Racial Equality, which challenged segregation in public transportation facilities throughout the heart of Dixie; and the nonviolent demonstrations of thousands of men, women, and children in the streets of Birmingham during spring 1963, mobilizing dissent in the "citadel of segregation."

We closely followed these dramatic events and were inspired to act in our own small community. We staged modest protest demonstrations in white-owned department stores and businesses in our downtown, demanding an end to racial segregation in hiring policies. Banks were pressured to extend credit and capital to blacks. The local newspapers and television stations, which had carefully ignored any coverage of the African-American community, gradually lifted the information blockade on blackness.

Oppressed people were mobilizing themselves in nonviolent civil disobedience. They registered new voters and organized Freedom Schools in shanties and churches across the rural South, transforming the political definition of what blackness could be. What I began to recognize in the relatively idealistic days of the early 1960s was that the powerful meaning and impact of "race" could be changed. As the struggle for power grew more intense, as Negroes boldly asserted themselves as never before, millions of white Americans were pressured and forced to re-examine their racist stereotypes and prejudices. Over time, most whites began to modify their language, their public behavior, and their treatment of black people in daily life. The schedules of public buses, which had never been routed through parts of the black community, were changed when I was a teenager, permitting us to travel downtown. Integration in the public secondary school I attended brought mixed and sometimes discouraging experiences. In one high school English class, the instructor required all students to memorize and recite

Rudyard Kipling's "White Man's Burden." Our social studies texts were devoid of references to Negroes; in our examination of "World Civilizations," Africa was not mentioned. But as black parents and students increasingly complained, modest changes were made in our curriculum.

The black freedom movement had permitted Negroes to perceive themselves as real actors in their own living history. The boundaries of what whites had defined as blackness were radically reinterpreted and renegotiated. In short, I came to recognize that race was no longer fixed, grounded in biological or genetic differences, or a natural division among human beings fostered through "cultural deprivation"; it was the logical consequence of structural power, structural privilege, and antiblack violence. As Negroes challenged and overthrew the institutions of racial inequality, the actual relationship between black and white was sharply altered. This is a historical lesson, from my own experience, that young people of color today must learn: Through their own direct action and struggle, constructive, meaningful change in contemporary racism is possible. We do not have to be passive victims of racism and intolerance. Rather, we must ever strive forward and seize every advantage that we can.

Riding high on the crest of the *Brown* wave, African Americans finally won access to higher education at unprecedented rates. In 1960, there were barely 200,000 African Americans enrolled in college, and three-fourths of that number attended historically black universities and colleges. By 1970, as a direct consequence of civil rights protests, 417,000 black Americans age 18 to 24 were attending college. Three-fourths of these new students were at predominantly white institutions. Five years later, 666,000 African Americans age 18 to 24 were enrolled in college, more than one out of every five blacks in their age group. Similar gains occurred at every level of education. The percentage of all African Americans completing four years of high school more than doubled in only fifteen years, from 20 percent in 1960 to 43 percent in 1975. The total number of African Americans under age 35 who held college degrees more than tripled in these same years, from 96,200 in 1960 up to 341,000 by 1975.

These unprecedented increases in educational access for black Americans were made possible, in part, by liberal public policies such as affirmative action, race-sensitive minority scholarship programs, and race-based recruitment efforts. Promising African-American high school students were offered "needs-blind" admissions packages, which made it financially possible for them to attend college. There was a general political consensus between both major parties at the time that "compensation" was due African Americans as a result of the legacy of legal racial segregation. One should keep in mind that the architects of these race-sensitive affirmative action policies were frequently Republicans, from Earl Warren to Richard M. Nixon.

In spite of the bipartisan support and a legal mandate from the Supreme Court, progress towards racial reform in the nation's public schools was painfully slow. As late as 1964, only about 2 percent of all African-American public school students across the South attended school with whites. According to a school segregation index developed by the Lewis Mumford Center at the University of Albany, as of 1968 93.1 percent of all black students in the Atlanta public school district would have had to relocate to other schools in order to achieve racial integration citywide. Other major U.S. cities had similarly high concentrations of racialized minorities. In Chicago, for example, 93.7 percent of African-American students would have had to move for integration in that city's school system; in Los Angeles, 93 percent; Miami (Dade County), 92.4 percent; Houston, 91.7 percent; St. Louis, 89.1 percent; Baltimore, 86.8 percent. Tens of millions of middle- to upper-class white households fled America's central cities partially to evade court-ordered school desegregation, relocating to the safe, white enclaves of suburbia in the 1960s and 1970s. White noncooperation and outright resistance was so blatant and undeniable that the U.S. Supreme Court, in *Griffin v. County School Board of Prince Edward County* in 1964, stated, "There has been entirely too much deliberation and not enough speed in enforcing the constitutional rights which we upheld in *Brown.*"

As black popular culture began to have a truly major impact on white, middle America in the 1970s, the majority of white Americans during those years did not overtly oppose affirmative action–type reforms that addressed blacks' historic disadvantages. However, one measure of how "liberal" the racial consensus actually was during the decade was the national debate over the *Bakke* decision of 1978. In a narrow five to four decision, the U.S. Supreme Court overturned the University of California at Davis's admissions program, which set aside a specific number, or quota, for minority applicants to be admitted. Writing for the majority, Associate Justice Lewis Powell rejected racial quotas, but strongly reaffirmed that the racial diversity of a student body comprised "a compelling state interest." As a necessary remedy for past discrimination, race could be legitimately used as a factor in awarding college scholarships and in other educational programs. At the time of the *Bakke* ruling, most African Americans saw this decision as a reactionary retreat from racial justice. Associate Justice Thurgood Marshall, in a vigorous dissent, angrily declared: "It must be remembered that, during most of the past 200 years, the Constitution as interpreted by this Court did not prohibit the most ingenious and pervasive forms of discrimination against the Negro. Now, when a State acts to remedy the effects of that legacy of discrimination, I cannot believe that this same Constitution stands as a barrier."

It is also crucial to remember, in today's era of "colorblind racism," that most of these rapid gains in African-American opportunities in education a generation ago coincided with the unprecedented expansion of the U.S. economy and declining unemployment rates. Between 1962 and 1969, overall jobless rates for African Americans declined from 10.9 percent to 6.4 percent. For black married males, unemployment rates dropped in these same years from 7.9 percent to 2.5 percent. The historic wage gap in median household incomes separating blacks and whites was reduced significantly, 50 to 60 percent. At the same time, the percentage of the black labor force classified as white-collar workers (e.g., professionals, technicians, clerical workers, managers) nearly doubled, from 13 percent to

24 percent, in only ten years. These economic factors played a major role in the push to restructure higher education to incorporate scholarship on the black experience. They also forced most whites to acknowledge that racial injustices towards blacks had been committed and that compensatory measures were necessary for the national interest.

During the eight years of the Reagan administration, both black studies programs and black access to higher education experienced some destabilization and decline. Ideologically, African-American studies programs and black cultural centers increasingly came under fierce attack as promoting "racial separatism," and in some notable cases "anti-Semitism." Reagan's Justice Department was overtly hostile to affirmative action, and the Equal Employment Opportunity Commission—headed by ambitious black conservative Clarence Thomas—essentially refused to enforce antidiscrimination laws. These political shifts had a negative impact on the number of blacks going to graduate and professional schools, as well as attending four-year colleges. But despite the destructiveness of the Reagan era, the socioeconomic balance sheet for African Americans, viewed from the historical perspective since World War II, still remained hopeful and positive.

Beginning in the late 1980s and through the mid-1990s, there was a second wave of sustained growth—nowhere near as spectacular as that of the 1960s and early 1970s, but substantial nevertheless. Universities that had resisted the creation of formal African-American studies departments or institutes, such as Columbia University, finally capitulated. Harvard University, which in 1989 had only one tenured faculty member in African-American studies, hired literary scholar Henry Louis Gates Jr. in 1991. In 1994, Harvard became home to the "Image of the Black in Western Art" photo archive, documenting fifty centuries of how people of African descent have been represented (and misrepresented) in Europe and North America. Gates and cultural studies scholar Anthony Appiah produced *Encarta Africana,* a comprehensive encyclopedic survey of African and African-American life and culture, which in some respects fulfilled W. E. B. Du Bois's vision of creating an *Encyclopedia Africana.*

Prominent public intellectual Cornel West and influential sociologist William Julius Wilson joined Gates's department in 1994 and 1996, respectively. It was Gates who dubbed his celebrated faculty "the Dream Team." *The New York Times* seemed to agree; *Times* education writer Peter Applebaum observed in 1996 that in only five years Gates had "raised $11 million for various black studies projects at Harvard. . . . Gates, et al will play a major role in finally taking African-American studies from an often marginalized and patronized field at the edges of the academy to its center."

During this second wave of sustained growth, universities and corporations began to promote what I have termed "corporate multiculturalism"—celebrating everyone while criticizing no one. "Diversity" became an institutional mantra, a value worthy of corporate endorsement and even the U.S. military's enthusiastic and uncritical support. Schools like Columbia doubled their budgets to recruit blacks, Latinos, and American Indians into their graduate schools. The

Mellon Foundation initiated a massive race-based fellow-ship program, identifying talented black and Latino under-graduate students and encouraging them to enter doctoral programs. By the late 1990s over one thousand Mellon Fel-lows, at more than three dozen institutions, had received hundreds of millions of dollars for summer stipends, travel expenses, tuition support, and debt forgiveness.

The Ford Foundation, after years of neglect, "rediscov-ered" its long dormant interest in black studies and began investing millions of dollars into key programs at the Uni-versity of Wisconsin, Cornell University, Harvard, and even City College of the City University of New York—once its controversial Afrocentric chair Leonard Jeffries was removed from his administrative post. The number of African Americans receiving professional degrees rose by 70 percent between 1989 and 2002. Likewise, black en-rollments in law schools jumped 50 percent between 1990 and 2000. Blacks earning Ph.D.s doubled in the decade, with 1,656 new doctorates produced in 2000.

The racial progress achieved in higher education during the 1980s and early to mid-1990s was paralleled, to a lesser extent, in many of America's public schools. In a sur-prising number of major urban school systems, the move-ment towards eliminating the hypersegregation of public schools in the 1980s was impressive. Boston, for example, the site of extremist white protests and violence against school desegregation, would have had to relocate 78.6 per-cent of its black students to achieve school integration in 1968. By 1990, that percentage had dropped significantly to 32.8 percent—lower than Seattle's desegregation ratio.

Other major cities experienced similar declines in the hypersegregation of their school systems. In Pittsburgh, the drop from 1968 to 1990 in the school segregation index was 74.2 percent to 40.5 percent; Cleveland, 89.4 percent to 22.7 percent; and Memphis, 80.5 percent down to 47.6 percent. Unfortunately these inspirational examples were merely exceptions, not the rule: The vast majority of American school districts remained overwhelmingly segregated by race, and increasingly stratified by class as well. Millions of white middle-class children continued to be pulled out of public schools. However, there was a sense that at least some interracial progress was being made in many of the nation's school districts. As millions of black and brown children slowly gained access to a quality education, they became more competitive scholastically and better prepared for these new higher educational opportunities.

It is curious that this "second wave" of black educational access took place at a time when the black freedom movement was in a period of severe decline, whereas the "first wave" was made possible by a strong leadership group made up of women and men like Robert Carter. The NAACP tottered near political irrelevance under the ineffectual leadership of Benjamin Hooks throughout the 1980s, and in 1993–1994 the Reverend Benjamin Chavis's brief, scandal-plagued tenure pushed the association near financial bankruptcy. Jesse Jackson, for reasons known only to him, deliberately dismantled his own Rainbow Coalition as a national, democratic resistance movement capable of challenging the neoliberal policies of both major parties. In 1995 Louis Farrakhan's Million Man March filled what had become a vast political vacuum in African-American politics, but both the Nation of Islam and most of the black nationalist–oriented forces that had participated in that successful mass mobilization lacked the political and organizational skills to construct a broad, ideologically diverse united front, which was necessary to attract significant sectors of the African-American public.

The failure of the Million Man March mobilization to consolidate a new model of black civil engagement weakened and demoralized the state of national black politics. Black activists on the left who had been critical of Farrakahan's mobilization attempted to build their own national network, as a counterweight to the patriarchy and homophobia that many of the Million Man March proponents had promoted. In 1998, about 2,000 African-American community organizers and intellectuals caucused in Chicago to launch the Black Radical Congress, which was conceived as a movement-oriented formation designed to promote new levels of activism against police brutality, privatization, and other repressive policies. Despite the Black Radical Congress's successful local campaigns in several major cities, it only survived as a national force for a few years as internal disputes and a lack of coherent organization led to its decline.

In retrospect, it seems to me that the social force behind this "second wave" of African-American access and expanding opportunity during the 1990s was the maturation of the African-American middle class, and especially the most affluent sectors of its professional, technical, and managerial elite. By the mid-1990s, the children of African Americans who had attended college largely on race-sensitive affirmative action scholarships were entering college. In *The Shape of the River: Long-Term Consequences of Considering Race in College and University Admissions,* authors William G. Bowen and Derek Bok, formerly presidents of Princeton and Harvard, respectively, acknowledged that affirmative action never substantially addressed or even recognized class inequality within black and Latino communities. Their survey of twenty-eight highly selective colleges and universities in the mid-1990s found that 86 percent of all black students enrolled were "middle class or upper middle class."

These statistics bear out the inherent class elitism that still overwhelmingly characterizes American higher education. According to the U.S. Census Bureau, as of 1998 in families with annual incomes above $75,000, 65 percent of their children between age 18 and 24 attend college. Only 24 percent of that same age group attend college from families earning under $25,000 annually. Research funded by the Century Foundation found that as of 2004, at the nation's 146 most selective colleges and universities, about 74 percent of all students came from households from the wealthiest socioeconomic quartile. Students from families in the lowest socioeconomic quartile currently make up only 3 percent of all students at these elite institutions. In terms of race, only about 30 percent of all African Americans age 18 to 24 attend college; for Latinos, the number drops to 20 percent.

The legacy of *Brown* had, in short, created the modern African-American professional and managerial class, and their children were able to take advantage of the institutional reforms that it had brought about. The architects of *Brown* did not, or could not, anticipate how entrenched the policies of "white racial preferences" were within higher education, in the form of special admissions treatment for the affluent. Thousands of "underqualified" white students from wealthy families, recommended by affluent donors, trustees, and alumni, continued to enter elite universities as "legacies," reducing opportunities for academically superior African-American, Latino, and working-class white students, thus preserving the hierarchy of white elite privilege. Most crucially, *Brown*'s legacy did not adequately or sufficiently address the steadily deepening crisis experienced by the children of the African-American working class and the poor. *Brown*'s failure to address the issue of class would loom large as the empire began to strike back.

If the victory of *Brown* laid the groundwork for modern class divisions within the African-American community, then one could also claim that the powerful rhetoric of the black freedom movement ironically had made possible the modern assault against black progress in higher education. Starting in the early 1990s, there was a dedicated, concerted effort by conservatives to literally turn the discourse of civil rights upside down. Their objective was, in effect, to rewrite the American public's memory about what had actually transpired in the 1950s and 1960s. Dr. Martin Luther King Jr.'s image and words were cynically manipulated in the national media to provide a posthumous endorsement for outlawing race-sensitive affirmative action programs. An important turning point occurred in California in November 1996, with the passage of Proposition 209,

the so-called "California Civil Rights Initiative." Winning
by a margin of 54 to 46 percent, the initiative outlawed the
use of "race, sex, color, ethnicity, or national origin" in
many aspects of public life.

Thousands of black and Latino voters, confused by the
language of the initiative, failed to understand that affirmative action would be outlawed in California, and voted
for it. On the day of the referendum, *Los Angeles Times*
exit polls indicated that a clear majority of California voters supported affirmative action programs. Yet these same
voters, confused or not, approved Proposition 209 and
made it state law. All of this was possible because the lessons and history of the Civil Rights Movement had been
largely erased from the national consciousness. As Ward
Connerly, the Negro conservative who led the campaign
for Proposition 209, explained: "The past is a ghost that
can destroy our future. It is dangerous to dwell upon it. To
focus on America's mistakes is to disregard its virtues."

White moderates and liberals who had long defended
race-based affirmative action programs waffled and largely
collapsed before the carefully orchestrated conservative on-
slaught. Setting the tone was President William Jefferson
Clinton, who in his re-election campaign of 1996 declared
that he had "done more to eliminate affirmative action programs I didn't think were fair and tighten others up than my
predecessors have since affirmative action has been around."
Clinton's failure to correctly frame the issue of affirmative
action around issues of U.S. racial history would prove decisive. In 1996, the U.S. Court of Appeals for the Fifth Circuit

in the *Hopwood v. State of Texas* decision outlawed the use of race as a factor in admissions to universities. Initiative 200 in Washington state in 1998 followed California in outlawing affirmative action enforcement.

Several states that overturned race-sensitive affirmative action programs in higher education adopted so-called "percentage plans" that were theoretically designed to maintain ethnic and racial diversity within university admissions without the use of "preferences." In Florida, Republican Governor Jeb Bush pushed through a voluntary ban on racial preferences by endorsing the plan to admit the top 20 percent of students in each Florida high school graduating class into one of the state's eleven public universities. Proponents of the "20 percent plan" argued that a "color-blind," across-the-board enrollment of high school students based on "merit" and "academic achievement" would generate significant numbers of black and Latino students from the hypersegregated public schools. Similar strategies were attempted in Texas and California. In Texas, the upper 10 percent of each high school's graduating class was automatically promised entry at Texas's public universities. In 2001, California began its 4 percent plan, which guaranteed admission for the top 4 percent of all graduating high school students to one of the University of California's nine institutions.

It didn't take long to find out that, as *The Chronicle of Higher Education* ruefully noted, the "'Percent Plans' don't add up." Under Florida's 20 percent admissions plan, black enrollment of first-year students in all state universities declined from 11.8 percent 2000 to only 7.2 percent in 2001; for Latinos in the same years, the decline was 12 percent to 11.1 percent. White enrollment in the state's freshman class surged from 66.3 percent in fall 2000 up to 72.3 percent in fall 2001.

At Texas A&M University, back in 1996 black and Latino in-state freshman enrollment comprised 3.4 percent and 11.5 percent, respectively, of the matriculating class; after the adoption of the 10 percent plan, by the fall of 2002, black and Latino freshman enrollments had fallen to 2.6 percent and 9.8 percent, respectively. The percentage of black in-state freshman admissions at the state's elite institution, University of Texas at Austin, declined from 4.4 percent in 1996 to 3.1 percent in 1998, then increased slightly to 3.5 percent by 2002.

In California, the record was somewhat more mixed. Institutions such as the University of California at Irvine stayed at roughly the same level from 1997 to 2001, even with the implementation of the 4 percent plan. At the University of California at Berkeley, however, African-American freshmen declined from 7.8 percent of all students in 1997, down to 3.9 percent by 2001. Latino first-year students matriculating at Berkeley also fell, 14.6 percent in 1997 down to 10.8 percent in 2001.

In June 2003, the U.S. Supreme Court decided two lawsuits involving race-sensitive affirmative action programs at the University of Michigan at Ann Arbor. The administration of President George W. Bush promptly filed briefs before the court, arguing that colleges should employ race-neutral means to achieve diversity. Bush's Justice Department's brief declared that Michigan "cannot justify the express consideration of race in the admissions policy," and to maintain such preferences was unconstitutional. Despite the Supreme Court's conservative majority, the court ruled against the Bush administration's position in the most important of the two decisions, *Grutter v. Bollinger*. In *Grutter*, the Supreme Court ruled that there was a compelling state interest in fostering programs enhancing "diversity," and that the quality of education was enriched by having individuals from different racial and ethnic backgrounds as part of a university environment. Therefore, the court declared in its narrow five to four ruling, the use of race as a factor was acceptable, so long as it was not applied as a quota. In effect, the Lewis Powell standard set in *Bakke* was deemed still constitutional. The initial response from the academic community was that *Grutter* represented a clear victory for the forces of affirmative action and "diversity." They unfortunately failed to comprehend the full weight of the majority's opinion on the high court: Universities had to consider prospective students henceforth "as individuals" and not reject or admit them through any programs that had the appearance of being based primarily or exclusively on racial categories.

The Supreme Court rulings also provided for twenty-five-year "sunset provisions," during which time colleges needed to move to "terminate race-conscious admissions program[s] as soon as practicable." Taken together, the *Gratz v. Bollinger* and *Grutter v. Bollinger* rulings actually strengthened the resolve of conservatives to pressure universities to outlaw any and all concessions to minority group access. In July 2003, only weeks after the University of Michigan rulings, Curt A. Levey of the conservative Center for Individual Rights, which represented the Michigan cases' plaintiffs, warned colleges and universities that "they would do well to cut the celebration short and begin planning now for the eventual phaseout of race-based admissions. Public opinion will demand it, voters and legislators may compel it, and continued litigation will necessitate it, long before the court's respite ends." A conservative group, the National Association of Scholars, began sending out freedom of information queries to state universities, demanding information about their use of "racial and ethnic preferences—particularly in admissions—and . . . whether the manner in which they do it is within the constraints set out by the Supreme Court in the University of Michigan cases," according to Roger Clegg, general counsel of the conservative Center for Equal Opportunity. Despite the legal victory of *Grutter*, Clegg predicted confidently that "the more that the use of preferences is made public, the less prevalent they will be." Furthermore, "*Gratz* and *Grutter* contain plenty of language that judges who are so inclined can cite in limiting the use of preferences." The net result was that many colleges and universities came to the conclusion that any programs or administrative offices they had established to support and sustain minority access and opportunity that could be interpreted as being primarily or exclusively designed on ethnic or racial criteria had to be eliminated.

In a brief period of time beginning in late 2003, hundreds of U.S. universities and colleges shut down or significantly transformed their minority-oriented programs. The list is truly stunning: At Yale University, a summer preregistration program for prefreshmen, "Cultural Connections," was opened to white participation; at Princeton University, all "race-exclusive programs" were halted, including its Junner Summer Institute, which annually brought African-American and Latino college students to the Woodrow Wilson School of Public and International Affairs. At Boulder, the University of Colorado's "Summer Minority Access to Research Training Program" was renamed and opened to whites. At the California Institute of Technology, its campus visit program designed for blacks, Latinos, and American Indians was opened to whites and Asian Americans. At Indiana University, the nine-week "Summer Minority Research Fellowship" originally designed "to get minority high school and college students interested in medical research by matching them with mentors" was restructured to recruit Asian Americans and whites. At St. Louis University, a scholarship program annually awarding $10,000 each to thirty African-American students was "disbanded" and substituted with the new "Martin Luther King Jr." scholarships, reduced to $8,000 per student, and accepting applications without consideration of race. And at Williams College in Massachusetts, a predoctoral fellowship program, which for more than a decade had awarded annually two to five general dissertation stipends to black and Latino advanced graduate students, with the original purpose of increasing minority professors, was radically opened to anyone regardless of color who is deemed "underrepresented," such as "women in physics departments," or "white applicants in Asian Studies." *Grutter* was no victory. It marked a cruel defeat that will reduce the opportunities for educational advancement for thousands of Latino and African-American students in the coming years, all in the name of "diversity."

Affirmative action policies were first crafted in reaction to the particular struggles and specific demands of the Civil Rights movement. The central issue, in the language of the day, was the status of the Negro in American society. Groups who were not originally part of the national debate over segregation, or who entered the country after the passage of the Civil Rights Act of 1964, materially benefited in real terms from blacks' sacrifices. By 2000, the overwhelming number of beneficiaries of affirmative action programs were non-black. In 2004 legal scholar Lani Guinier estimated that the vast majority of the beneficiaries of minority-oriented admissions programs at Harvard University were not native-born African Americans.

In 1995, two years after my arrival at Columbia University, I convinced the administration to create a standing Minority Affairs Committee for the graduate school, and to substantially increase its scholarship funds for "under-represented minorities" in Ph.D. programs. Increasingly, individuals who by traditional U.S. standards would be considered "white" demanded financial support on distant and even fictive connections with American Indian, Hispanic, Caribbean, and African-American heritages. Several Asian Americans, who as a group are underrepresented in some humanities disciplines, began demanding race-based scholarships for the humanities. Some "biracial" individuals attempted to make a case for themselves as a special discriminated class worthy of relief. Well-meaning but confused white faculty at Columbia quietly petitioned the graduate school for funds to recruit outstanding prospective students from Argentina, Chile, Uruguay, China, Spain, Japan, or other nations, with the objective of "enhancing diversity" within their department's doctoral program. With growing frustration, I was repeatedly called upon to deliver a mini–history lesson to my wavering colleagues, explaining that the original purpose of affirmative action was to redress the continuing effects and consequences of U.S. legal racialization, aimed specifically against African Americans, Puerto Ricans, American Indians, and Mexican Americans for several centuries. My arguments carried the weight of history, but the prevailing attitude of white liberal academicians was increasingly to divorce the past from the present.

Affirmative action was a beneficial reform that could have worked well long-term only if "race" stood still. It doesn't. Race is a dynamic, changing social relationship grounded in structural inequality. As the human composition of American society's social order has shifted, the lived reality of structural racism has also changed in everyday existence. What has remained constant, unfortunately, is that "blackness," no matter how it is constituted in ethnic terms, has continued to be stigmatized and relegated to the periphery of power and opportunity. The liberal multiculturalists who now "celebrate diversity," devoid of any historical appreciation of structural racism in the construction of modern America, actually perpetuate racialized inequality today by their refusal to bear witness to the truths of our shared past. White liberals are unwilling or unable to question the dispossession of wealth from African Americans in the form of unpaid labor exploitation throughout centuries of black enslavement and oppression under Jim Crow segregation. The liberal language of diversity obscures the continuing burden of racialized lives that blacks still endure.

In addition to affirmative action's inability to adjust to the fluid realities of race in America, it has also never meaningfully addressed the economic foundations of structural racism. As political scientist Ronald Walters has observed, affirmative action was essentially "paycheck equality." It gave millions of mostly middle-class, better-educated African Americans opportunities for career advancement. It did not fundamentally alter the racial inequality in wealth ownership within U.S. society. The average African-American household today has only 7 percent of the net wealth of the average white household. One-third of all black families actually have a negative net wealth.

The growing problem of inequality, to be sure, is not an exclusively racial issue in itself. Researchers Stacie Carney and William G. Gale estimate that fully one-fourth of all U.S. households have virtually no financial assets; 20 percent have no savings or checking accounts; and about one-half of all American families have under $5,000 in total financial assets. The argument that the majority of Americans are comfortably part of an affluent middle class is flat-out wrong. But the racial element has never been incidental in the structural arrangements of U.S. society. The lack of asset accumulation has been severely crippling to the development of all kinds of African-American institutions and communities as a whole. Affirmative action as an approach to racial reform did not address the necessary transfer of wealth needed to materially develop black communities. Only reparations could have begun to address this.

The dismantling of minority affairs programs, affirmative action–inspired scholarships, and minority student summer training programs at universities coincided with what could be called the resegregation of many major public school districts by 2000. In a host of cities where significant progress had been achieved in desegregating schools, that progress was rapidly pushed back in the ideological environment of hostility to affirmative action. Again using the Lewis Mumford Center's school segregation index, in 2000, 81.7 percent of New York City's African-American schoolchildren would have had to be relocated to achieve greater racial balance, a figure higher than in 1968 (72.2 percent). In Cleveland, where the school segregation index had declined to 22.7 percent in 1990, the city witnessed a steep rise (72.9 percent) by 2000. A similar dynamic of increased racial concentration in the public schools occurred in Seattle, Denver, Houston, San Francisco, and Pittsburgh.

The trends of exclusion and isolation for a new generation of black schoolchildren were so deep and profound that even Rod Paige, George W. Bush's conservative Secretary of Education, was forced to acknowledge them. "We face an emerging de facto apartheid in our schools, a contemporary crisis that is similar, perhaps identical, to the situation in the 1950s South," Paige declared in 2004. He added that "we must address it with the same vision, commitment and courage found in *Brown v. Board of Educa-*

tion." More pessimistically, historian John Hope Franklin delivered a eulogy for the death of *Brown's* promise: "There's no program, no grand dream or idea that in 2005, 2015, or 2020 that we will have no more segregation of schools. . . . Behind that, there is no more dream of equality, of access to the facilities and resources that could be available to every child and adult in this country." The collapse of any coordinated effort to desegregate America's public schools has forced blacks to reconsider the legacy of *Plessy.* Is it possible under the current conditions of "neo-apartheid" for ghetto youth to receive an "equal education" with upper-middle-class whites? Since the majority of white Americans now claim to love "diversity," yet reject race-sensitive affirmative action, what practical remedies could be sought that could effectively reduce the racial divide? Millions of middle- to upper-class white Americans have reconstructed Jim Crow barriers by creating exclusive suburban enclaves and gated communities, where it is once again possible to dwell in the racial cocoon of whiteness, encountering blacks mostly in subservient positions, as household, maintenance, and security personnel. Their children may be captivated with hip-hop culture, but that has little impact on the changing racially restrictive residential patterns that preserve whites' real estate values.

Putting the future in greater jeopardy, the rising group of young, middle-class African American professionals—the second and third post-Brown generations—seems in my judgment ill-prepared for the post–affirmative action era looming ahead. Many are so disconnected from social protest movements and the historical struggles of their own people that they are unable to comprehend what is actually happening in the public policy arena. In higher education, some have come to the bizarre belief that their personal career advancement is based exclusively on their own "merit," and that the severe reductions in the numbers of black graduate students, undergraduates, administrators, and faculty will not personally affect their future career prospects. Others do worry about the loss of affirmative action, but only from the perspective of the reduction of potential career opportunities for themselves.

Even those young African-American intellectuals who have liberal and progressive political views generally lack any theoretical grounding, and likely have little intimate experience working with black working-class and grassroots mass-style organizations. Subsequently, they cannot fashion any appropriate plan for constructively engaging in the current struggles being waged in poor neighborhoods all over the nation. This is, in many ways, the first black generation adrift from its own rich history of collective struggle.

Paradoxically, affirmative action itself, and more generally the philosophy of liberal integrationism, contributed to this widespread historical amnesia and color-blindness among many Generation X blacks. Integration as a strategy for achieving racial justice rarely asked black people what kind of American society they wanted; it only promoted pragmatic reforms that our existing structure could permit us to achieve. Integration emphasized individual opportunity and symbolic representation, rather than the removal of the deep structural barriers that perpetuated inequality. Integrationists usually spoke a language of the nation-state, rather than a discourse of internationalism and pan-Africanism.

In electoral politics, integrationists placed their faith in the national Democratic Party and in the old New Deal–Great Society style coalitions to deliver public programs and policies that would empower the black community. They never comprehended that what was required was an "inside-outside" approach to power: building strong black institutions and employing independent electoral campaigns wherever possible to pressure Democratic administrations into greater accountability to blacks' interests. Still, the greatest weakness, conceptually and politically, of the integrationists was their failure to plan strategically beyond the demise of Jim Crow segregation. They did not anticipate the erection of an even more powerful "racial domain," a system of racialized economy, warehousing more than one million blacks in prisons, and disfranchising millions more. An oppressed people without total recall of their own history of exploitation and resistance cannot craft a new history of liberation.

The quest for "freedom," as African Americans have defined it through their myriad struggles for dignity and collective capacity-building, has always involved two core ideals: equality and self-determination. Equality—the achievement of full civil and democratic rights under the existing U.S. state and the abolition of all structural barriers based on racial designation—was largely the focus of the liberal integrationists. Self-determination is a concept directly linked to the historical fact citizenship was defined in distinctly racial terms for hundreds of years. The material oppression of African Americans has been carried out by the whole of white society, including white workers and the poor. Consequently, black people have an inalienable right to determine their own future, regardless of whatever political institutions we live under. This is the ideological kernel of the black nationalist tradition in the United States.

Both of these historic tendencies within the black freedom struggle have been made largely obsolete by globalization, the vast transformation of America's racial and ethnic composition, privatization, and growing class stratification within the black community itself. Put more simply, could Elijah Muhammad's Nation of Islam or the Republic of New Afrika's concept of a separate black state, the "Black Belt Nation," have credibility in the twenty-first century, when multinational corporations are surpassing most nations in their ability to define the economic realities of the lives of most people on the planet? What viability does "integration" retain, given the dismantling of minority economic set-asides and the near-elimination of race-sensitive affirmative action reforms? This is not an abstract exercise, but a call for connecting theory with practice. Even the interdisciplinary scholarship in black studies, in both its Afrocentric and liberal multiculturalist variants, has largely drifted toward becoming an academic commodity, more like an aesthetic museum than a social laboratory for scientific investigation in the Du Boisian tradition. It must refocus its energies on the concrete conditions and the difficult contradictions that constitute the stuff of daily life of African Americans, as well as other people of African descent transnationally.

The old ideologies that have defined African-American political culture are outmoded precisely because the so-called stuff of daily life is qualitatively different than it was a generation ago. A color-blind new racial domain has emerged in the United States in the post–Civil Rights era. This is not a restoration of Jim Crow segregation, but the reconfiguration of deep-seated structures of power. The new racial domain is constructed as a deadly triangle (or perhaps, an "unholy trinity") of structural racism: mass unemployment, mass incarceration, and mass disfranchisement. This deadly triangle of color-blind racialization creates an endless cycle of economic marginalization, stigmatization, and social exclusion, culminating in civil and social death for millions of Americans.

The cycle of destruction starts with chronic, mass unemployment and poverty. Real incomes for the working poor actually fell significantly during Clinton's second term in office. After the 1996 welfare reform, the social safety net was largely dismantled. As the Bush administration took power, chronic joblessness spread to black workers in the manufacturing sector. By 2003 in New York City nearly one-half of all black male adults were outside of the paid labor force. A 2005 study by the John Jay College of Criminal Justice found that in New York City white males with prison records receive significantly more job offers for entry-level positions than African Americans who have never been arrested. Black men who have served time in prison were only about one-third as likely as whites with similar criminal records to receive call-backs after submitting applications for a wide number of jobs, from deli clerks to telemarketers.

This sort of mass unemployment inevitably feeds the trend of mass incarceration. About one-fourth of all prisoners are unemployed at the time of their arrests, and others averaged less than $20,000 annual incomes in the year prior to their incarceration. When the Attica prison insurrection occurred in upstate New York in 1971, there were only 12,500 prisoners in New York's correctional facilities and about 300,000 prisoners nationwide. By 2001, New York held over 71,000 women and men in its prisons; nationally, 2.1 million were imprisoned. Today about five to six million Americans are arrested annually, and roughly one in six Americans possess a criminal record. Mandatory-minimum sentencing laws adopted in the 1980s and 1990s have stripped judges of their discretionary powers in sentencing, and mandate draconian terms for first-time and nonviolent offenders. Meanwhile, parole has been made more restrictive, and Pell grant subsidies supporting educational programs for prisoners were ended in 1995. Those fortunate enough to successfully navigate the criminal justice bureaucracy and emerge from incarceration discover that both the federal and state governments explicitly prohibit the employment of convicted ex-felons in hundreds of vocations. The cycle of unemployment starts all over again.

In seven states, as of 2005, former prisoners convicted of a felony lose their voting rights for life. In the majority of states, individuals on parole and probation cannot vote. About 13 percent of all African-American males nationally are either permanently or currently disfranchised. In Mississippi, one-third of all black men are unable to vote for the remainder of their lives. In Florida, 818,000 residents cannot vote for life. Even temporary disfranchisement fosters a disruption of civic engagement and involvement in public affairs. This can lead to "civil death," and this process of depolitization undermines even grassroots, non-electoral-oriented organizing. The deadly triangle of the new racial domain will continuously grow if left unchecked.

The political impact of mass incarceration reduces black and Latino voting power in other ways as well. In New York, for example, two-thirds of all prisoners in the state's penal institutions were residents of New York City; however, all of New York's forty-three new correctional facilities constructed since 1976 have been located in upstate New York, in traditionally Republican constituencies. In racial and ethnic terms, about 82 percent of New York's prison population is black or Latino, but 98 percent of all state prisons are located in Republican state senate districts that are predominantly white. Prisoners cannot vote, yet their numbers are counted as part of the residential population for determining boundaries for state legislative districts. Minority representation in New York's state legislature is thereby diminished, while white Republican constituencies benefit from their prisoner populations. A similar situation of racialized disfranchisement through outsourcing prisoners to white rural areas exists throughout the United States, according to the research of Peter

Wagner of the Prison Policy Initiative of the Open Society Institute (Soros Foundation). In Illinois, 60 percent of the state's prisoners are Cook County (Chicago) residents, yet 99 percent of all state correctional facilities are outside of Cook County. Over one-third of all state prisoners in California are residents of Los Angeles County, but only 3 percent of all prisoners are housed there. The vast majority of the nation's 2.1 million prisoners, most of whom cannot vote, are warehoused in largely white, Republican districts, significantly increasing conservative political representation at the expense of urban, heavily minority districts.

Not too far in the distance lies the social consequence of these destructive policies: an unequal, two-tiered, uncivil American society, characterized by a governing hierarchy of middle- to upper-class "citizens." These elites will own nearly all property and financial assets, while a vast population of racialized outcasts and the dispossessed struggle beneath the cruel weight of permanent unemployment, discriminatory courts and sentencing procedures, dehumanized prisons, voting disfranchisement, residential segregation, and the elimination of most public services for the poor. The disfranchised, dispossessed class is already virtually excluded from any influence in national, state, and local public policy. Meanwhile, democratic institutions that once provided space for upward mobility and resistance on behalf of working people, such as unions, have already been largely dismantled. Integral to all of this is racism, sometimes openly vicious and unambiguous, but much more frequently presented in race-neutral, color-blind language. The logic of *Brown* has successfully been turned upside down.

How can we still fulfill the promise of *Brown*? We must begin by building popular resistance to the new racial domain. We may, for the sake of historical continuity, call this the "New Civil Rights Movement" for the twenty-first century. Although history never repeats itself, the lessons of popular resistance and the tactics used for the creative, non-violent disruption that were employed in the 1950s and 1960s must be taught again and learned by a new generation of Americans. Hopeful signs exist that resistance is already occurring, on the ground, in thousands of venues. People are fighting against police brutality in local neighborhoods, against mandatory-minimum sentencing laws, and for prisoners' rights. Workers across the globe are fighting for a living wage, to expand unionization, for health care, for public transportation, for decent housing, and for affordable day care for their children. These struggles are the core of day-to-day resistance. Building up hope and cooperation within racially diverse neighborhoods to achieve practical and meaningful reforms develops our ability to resist and challenge the new racial domain in direct ways.

The successful Immigrant Worker Freedom Ride in 2004, highlighting the plight of undocumented workers who enter the United States, represents an excellent model that links the oppressive situation of new immigrants with the historic struggles of the Civil Rights movement. White activists who believe in racial justice can contribute to this unfolding struggle by learning more about the historic black freedom movement. The Civil Rights movement provides successful models of resistance—from selective buying campaigns or economic boycotts, to rent strikes, to civil disobedience—that are still viable today. By studying and learning from the mistakes and errors of past movements, we can acquire invaluable lessons for today's struggles. Similarly, a deeper knowledge and appreciation of parallel struggles for racial justice internationally can empower our capacity to resist here in the United States.

The national debate over *Brown*'s legacy and affirmative action is only part of a much larger global struggle for racial justice. In China, for example, students from that country's officially recognized fifty-five ethnic minority groups receive extra points on national entrance examination scores for university admissions. In India, about one-half of all seats for university entrance are set aside for historically disadvantaged groups. In Brazil, the Rio de Janeiro state legislature in 2001 approved legislation establishing quotas of 50 percent for graduates of public high schools, and 40 percent for black or *pardo* students for entrance into the two universities under its authority. The challenge of reversing the centuries-old patterns of racialized discrimination and exclusion of minority populations is not going away anytime soon.

Robert Carter was never under any illusions about how challenging the struggle against structural racism was, and how difficult it would be for African Americans to establish and sustain effective alliances to change public policies. In Carter's words, he realized "that black people could not rely on any white institution in this country to assert their rights, when such assertion was or appeared to be in conflict with a powerful competing white interest." In 2004, Carter was awarded the NAACP's Spingarn Medal, marking, among other things, his central role in the *Brown* decision a half century earlier. Carter recognizes *Brown* as a "pivotal moment in the struggle for racial justice. It launched the movement that overturned Jim Crow in the South and sparked a revolution in black consciousness and race relations, one that transformed America's social and political landscape and continues to resonate to this day." Yet the reality of racial inequality endures, and the dynamics of racialized oppression for millions of poor and economically marginalized blacks are even worse today relative to whites than a half century ago. For Carter, the challenge before us is clear: "The struggle to make equality for all people a fundamental tenet in our society continues; the meaning and dynamic legacy of *Brown* provide the foundation for activists and scholars committed to fulfilling its promise."

The examples of Robert Carter, Charles Hamilton Houston, and Thurgood Marshall set into bold relief for us the political courage and selfless dedication that will be required to achieve that final victory over structural racism in today's America. These principled advocates of civil rights effectively used the courts and the political process to force this nation to implement its own constitutional democratic principles on behalf of all its citizens. That same willingness to directly challenge the institutions of racialized inequality must inform the building of a New Civil Rights Movement for social and racial justice, in our own time. It is our living legacy to fulfill the long deferred promise of *Brown* by transcending its intellectual and political limitations. By understanding and bearing witness to that history, we may begin to live a new history.

Notes

Chapter 1

1 "which can sustain the present and prefigure possibility": Edward Thompson, "The Politics of Theory," quoted in James Green, *Taking History to Heart: The Power of the Past in Building Social Movements* (Amherst: University of Massachusetts Press, 2000), p. 25.

5 "hole, our private consciousness on manhood": Manning Marable, *Blackwater: Historical Studies in Race, Class Consciousness and Revolution* (Dayton, Ohio: Black Praxis, 1981), pp. 15–16.

5 no compensation given to the "lost generation" or their descendants: In Jim Carrier, *Traveler's Guide to the Civil Rights Movement* (New York: Harcourt, 2004), pp. 49–50.

6 "and political anger about police brutality": See Manning Marable, *The Great Wells of Democracy: The Meaning of Race in American Life* (New York: Basic Civitas, 2002), pp. 210, 304.

8 "biggest slave traders in the American colonies": "Brown University to Consider Reparations on Account of the Institution's Past Ties to Slavery," *Journal of Blacks in Higher Education*, no. 43 (Spring 2004), p. 18. Also see Pam Belluck, "Brown U to Examine Debt to Slave Trade," *New York Times*, March 13, 2004; and Tatsha Robertson and Ross Kerber, "History Unchained: Delving Beyond Celebrated Abolitionists, New Englanders Are Unearthing Painful Family Roots in the African Slave Trade," *Boston Globe*, August 6, 2000. Brown University's University Hall, which currently

houses the office of its president, was also originally constructed with a labor crew that included several black slaves.

8 **"Basking Ridge, New Jersey, throughout the Revolutionary War"**: Marilyn H. Pettit, "Slavery, Abolition, and Columbia University," *Journal of Archival Organization,* vol. 1, no. 4 (2002), pp. 80, 84.

9 **opposed the slave trade and slavery's expansion**: Ibid., pp. 77–89. To Duer's credit, despite his extensive family ties to African slavery, throughout his public career he opposed slavery. In 1790 Duer endorsed petitions by Pennsylvania Quakers and by a group led by Benjamin Franklin demanding the end of the trans-Atlantic slave trade. See Pettit, "Slavery, Abolition, and Columbia University," p. 85.

9 **had with African-American slavery**: See Randall Robinson, *The Debt: What America Owes to Blacks* (New York: Plume, 2000).

9 **"$5 million scholarship for African Americans in Louisiana"**: Jason B. Johnson, "Firms that Profited from Slavery Reviewed; Richmond, Oakland Consider Early Step to Seeking Reparations," *San Francisco Chronicle,* March 12, 2005.

10 **"experience of African Americans in our country"**: Laura Smitherman, "Wachovia Apologizes for Slavery Ties of Predecessors," *Baltimore Sun,* June 2, 2005. Wachovia Bank's disclosures were compelled by Chicago's 2000 ordinance requiring companies doing business there to reveal past links to slavery.

11 **nation's largest public pension system**: Johnson, "Firms That Profited from Slavery Reviewed."

11 **systematic discrimination against African Americans**: Claudia H. Deutsch, "Race Remains a Difficult Issue for Many Workers at Kodak," *New York Times,* August 24, 2004.

12 **has now become "Memorial Hall"**: "Vanderbilt University Abandons Effort to Remove the Word 'Confederate' from a Campus Building," *Journal of Blacks in Higher Education Weekly Bulletin,* July 21, 2005.

13 **little time in denouncing her bold initiative**: See Andrea L. Foster and Alyson Klein, "Brown U. to Explore Slavery,

Reparations," *Chronicle of Higher Education,* vol. 50, no.
29 (March 25, 2004), p. A30; Pam Belluck, "Brown U. to
Examine Debt to Slave Trade," *New York Times,* March 13,
2004; Adrian Walker, "Brave Inquiry for Brown," *Boston
Globe,* March 15, 2004; and DeWayne Wickham, "President of Brown Seeks to Fuel Reparations Debate," *USA Today,* March 16, 2004.

13   **"and Jesse Jackson are up front":** Thomas Sowell, "Rattling
the Chains," *Human Events,* vol. 60, no. 11 (March 29,
2004), p. 14.

14   **earliest presidents also owned slaves:** Foster and Klein,
"Brown U. to Explore Slavery Reparations."

15   **people suffer and their attempts to overcome them:** C. L. R.
James, "Black People in the Urban Areas of the United
States," in Anna Grimshaw, ed., *The C. L. R. James Reader*
(Oxford: Blackwell, 1992), pp. 375–378.

17   **few means to reconstruct these crimes:** Marable, *The Great
Wells of Democracy,* p. 41.

17   **around the charred corpse for souvenir photographs:** See
Manning Marable and Leith Mullings, *Freedom: A Photographic History of the African American Struggle* (London:
Phaiden, 2002), p. 101.

18   **pointing proudly to one of the dangling corpses:** Ibid.,
p. 132.

18   **"back to jail, which was just a half-block away":** Sheryl Gay
Stolberg, "Senate Issues Apology over Failure on Anti-Lynching Law," *New York Times,* June 14, 2005.

19   **John Sununu (R-New Hampshire), and Craig Thomas
(R-Wyoming):** "Eight U.S. Senators Decline to Cosponsor
Resolution Apologizing for Failure to Enact Anti-Lynching
Legislation," *Journal of Blacks in Higher Education Weekly
Bulletin,* June 30, 2005; and Avis Thomas-Lester, "Repairing
Senate's Record on Lynching," *Washington Post,* June 11,
2005.

23   **"you find yourself facing the whole nation":** C. L. R. James,
"Black People in the Urban Areas of the United States,"
pp. 375–378.

25   "claim as their own during Reconstruction": Ira Berlin, Marc Favreau, and Steven F. Miller, eds., *Remembering Slavery: African Americans Talk About Their Personal Experiences of Slavery and Freedom* (New York: The New Press, 1998), p. xiv.

27   "geology, the selective sedimentation of past traces": Popular Memory Group, "Popular Memory: Theory, Politics, Method," in Richard Johnson, Gregor McLennan, Bill Schwarz, and Richard Sutton, eds., *Making Histories: Studies in History-Writing and Politics* (London: Hutchinson, 1987), p. 205–252.

27   "the complicated character of their recollections": Robin D. G. Kelley, "Foreword," in Berlin, Favreau, and Miller, eds., *Remembering Slavery*, p. viii.

27   they themselves had learned as children: Ibid., pp. xiv, xix.

28   and other efforts as "preserving living history": John W. Fountain, "Finding Black History's Lost Stories," *New York Times,* December 29, 2002.

29   "revenge has no place in politics": C. L. R. James, *The Black Jacobins* (New York: Penguin, 2001), p. 301.

30   "civil rights activists were killed": See Len Holt, *The Summer That Didn't End: The Story of the Mississippi Freedom Summer* (New York: Da Capo Press, 1964); Doug McAdam, *Freedom Summer* (New York: Oxford University Press, 1988); John Rachal, "The Long, Hot Summer: The Mississippi Response to Freedom Summer, 1964," *Journal of Negro History,* vol. 84, no. 3 (Autumn 1999), p. 315–339; and Sally Belfrage, *Freedom Summer* (New York: Viking Press, 1966).

30   "the mills that produced the region's wealth": Green, *Taking History to Heart*, p. 151.

34   "to make history turn out differently": Paul B. Miller, "Counterfactual History: Not 'What If' but 'Why Not?'" *Chronicle of Higher Education,* vol. 50, no. 23 (February 13, 2004), pp. B10–B11.

35   "savings were exported to Florida and elsewhere": Mike Davis, *Dead Cities and Other Tales* (New York: The New Press, 2002), p. 389.

36 "hidden history of structural racism is revealed": Ibid, p. 364.

36 "given and transmitted from the past": Karl Marx, "The Eighteenth Brumaire of Louis Bonaparte," in K. Marx, F. Engels, and V. I. Lenin, eds. *On Historical Materialism* (New York: International Publishers, 1974), p. 120.

Chapter 2

39 "role of *conscious purpose* drawn from values": James MacGregor Burns, *Leadership* (New York: Harper and Row, 1978), p. 143.

41 "enclosed by America's expanding borders": Ronald Takaki, *A Different Mirror: A History of Multicultural America* (Boston: Little, Brown and Company, 1993), pp. 7, 16, 154.

43 "these United States at this very hour": Fredrick Douglass, "What to the Slave is the Fourth of July?" in Alice Moore Dunbar, ed., *Masterpieces of Negro Eloquence* (New York: Bookery Publishing, 1914), pp. 42–47.

44 "which the white man was bound to respect": See Manning Marable, *The Great Wells of Democracy: The Meaning of Race in American Life* (New York: Basic Civitas, 2002), p. 35.

45 holding elective office anywhere in the country: Ibid., pp. 41–48, 69–70. The Democratic Party's central role in preserving the Jim Crow system explains why, even a generation after Franklin Roosevelt's New Deal and the rise of modern liberalism within the party, significant numbers of blacks who were at that time permitted to vote supported the Republicans. Even Richard M. Nixon, for example, received a decent 32 percent of the black vote in the presidential election of 1960 (ibid., p. 70).

49 "ever attended their history on this continent!": Alexander Crummell, *Africa and America: Addresses and Discourses* (Springfield, Mass.: Wiley and Company, 1891), pp. 85–125.

50 Juneteenth in a resolution passed in 1997: Avis Thomas-Lester, "For Many, Today Is Independence Day," *Washington Post*, June 18, 2005.

52 "of the older selves to be lost": W. E. B. Du Bois, *The Souls of Black Folk* (Chicago: A. C. McClurg, 1903).

54 "stand there simply lost in admiration of my hair looking 'white'": Malcolm X, *The Autobiography of Malcolm X* (New York: Grove Press, 1965), p. 56.

55 "concepts, and try to set afoot a new man": Frantz Fanon, *The Wretched of the Earth* (New York: Grove Press, 1963), pp. 315–316.

55 "a spokesman for Negroes—and a Negro leader": Malcolm X, *Malcolm X Speaks* (New York: Grove Weidenfeld, 1963), p. 13.

57 "'permanent persuader' and not just a simple orator": Antonio Gramsci's discussion of the formation and social function of intellectuals is found in *Selections from the Prison Notebooks of Antonio Gramsci*, edited and translated by Quintin Hoare and Geoffrey Nowell Smith (New York: International Publishers, 1973), pp. 3–23.

58 collective struggle, social analysis with social transformation: See Manning Marable, ed., *Dispatches from the Ebony Tower: Intellectuals Confront the African American Experience* (New York: Columbia University Press, 2000), pp. 1–2.

62 scientific facts that had seemed completely fixed: See Silvio Bergia, "Einstein and the Birth of Special Relativity," in A. P. French, ed., *Einstein: A Centenary Volume* (Cambridge: Harvard University Press, 1979), pp. 65–89.

63 "a foundation quite different from the Newtonian": Albert Einstein, "On the Method of Theoretical Physics," in French, *Einstein: A Centenary Volume,* pp. 310–314. Einstein added, "But quite apart from the question of the superiority of one or the other, the fictitious character of the fundamental principles is perfectly evident from the fact that we can point to two essentially different principles, both of which correspond with experience to a large extent; this proves at the same time that every attempt at a logical deduction of the basic concepts and postulates of mechanics from elementary experiences is doomed to failure" (p. 312).

Chapter 3

67 **"gambling on television and even in churches"**: W. E. B. Du Bois, "The Negro and Socialism," in Helen Alfred, ed., *Toward a Socialist* America (New York: Peace Publications, 1958), pp. 179–191.

67 **"the colour line, in a wider context"**: C. L. R. James, *The Future in the Present* (Westport, Conn.: Lawrence Hill, 1980), p. 212.

68 **at each individual place setting**: Luther Keith, "NAACP Speaker Gives Straight Talk on Racism," *Detroit News*, May 1, 2003. Also see Orlandar Brand-Williams, "Scholar at Freedom Fund Event," *Detroit News*, April 16, 2003; and Orlandar Brand-Williams, "NAACP Should Broaden Reach, Activist Says," *Detroit News*, April 28, 2003.

70 **"later years Dr. Du Bois chose another path"**: Manning Marable, *W. E. B. Du Bois: Black Radical Democrat* (Boston: Twayne Publishers, 1986), p. 214.

72 **"who espoused or acted upon it"**: "The Souls of Black Folk: 100 Years Later" (brochure celebrating the Forty-Eighth Annual Fight for Freedom Fund Dinner, Detroit, Mich., April 27, 2003).

74 **Du Bois in the first place was desired**: Other significant conferences or public programs devoted to *The Souls of Black Folk* were sponsored by the University of Wisconsin—Madison, Oberlin College, the University of Virginia, the University of North Carolina, the University of California—Riverside, and Miami University of Ohio. See "UC Riverside Celebrates Centennial of 'Souls of Black Folk,'" University of California—Riverside news release, April 23, 2003, www.newsroom.ucr.edu; Deborah Kong, "100 Years After Publication, 'Souls of Black Folk' Resonates," Associated Press, April 22, 2003, www.zwire.com/site/news; and Lynne Duke, "A Searing Century for the Black Soul," *Washington Post*, April 27, 2003, p. D1.

75 **on behalf of African and Caribbean countries**: Felicia R. Lee, "A Challenge to White Supremacy, 100 Years Later;

Scholars Revisit W. E. B. Du Bois, Who Found a New Way to Think About Race in America," *New York Times,* April 15, 2003.

75 **final forty years of Du Bois' public life:** Beth Potier, "'The Souls of Black Folk': Du Bois Institute Commemorates Centenary of Namesake's Landmark Work with Readings, Sons," *Harvard Gazette,* May 1, 2003, www.news.harvard. edu/gazette/2003/05.01/09-souls.html.

76 **observed Anica Butler in the *Hartford Courant*:** Anica Butler, "Dual-Identity Perspective of 'Black Folk' Still Relevant," *Hartford Courant,* February 16, 2003.

76 **America of the twenty-first century:** Duke, "A Searing Century for the Black Soul."

77 **"his U.S. Citizenship" and died in Ghana:** "Du Bois' Accomplishments Deserve to be Emphasized," *Nashville City Paper,* April 29, 2003.

77 **"embassy refused to renew his passport":** David Levering Lewis, *W. E. B. Du Bois: The Fight for Equality and the American Century, 1919–1963* (New York: Henry Holt and Company, 2001), p. 569.

78 **views of Washington and Du Bois:** "Tribute to W. E. B. Du Bois' *Souls of Black Folk,*" *Tavis Smiley Show,* National Public Radio, April 17, 2003.

78 **with Du Bois holding "the opposite view":** John Bloom, "Assignment America: 'Souls of Black Folk,'" United Press International, April 25, 2003. In this muddled, poorly written essay, Bloom questions whether Du Bois, who was so knowledgeable about "the great ideas of the West," could "really become a citizen of Ghana in his heart? . . . Did he cast aside all these things for a fierce 'back to Africa' black separatism? Did he come to believe that America could be America without her Negro people?" Bloom in effect merges Du Bois with Marcus Garvey.

78 **"influence on all aspects of human science":** Robin D. G. Kelley, quoted in Duke, "A Searing Century for the Black Soul."

79 **"of being black in post–Civil War America":** Stuart Hall, "Tearing Down the Veil," (London) *Guardian,* February 22, 2003.

79   **"this country since *Uncle Tom's Cabin"*:** James Weldon Johnson, *Along This Way* (New York: Viking, 1935), p. 203.

81   **"taste, great moderation and almost contemptuous fairness":** W. E. B. Du Bois, "Jefferson Davis as a Representative of Civilization," commencement address, June 25, 1890, in Herbert Aptheker, ed., *Against Racism: Unpublished Essays, Papers, Addresses, 1887–1961* (Amherst: University of Massachusetts Press, 1985), pp. 16–17.

81   **examination of race and racism in an urban context:** See W. E. B. Du Bois, *The Philadelphia Negro: A Social Study, Together with a Special Report on Domestic Service* by Isobel Eaton (Philadelphia: University of Pennsylvania, 1899).

83   **"all things essential to mutual progress":** Booker T. Washington, "Up from Slavery" (first published 1901), in *Three Negro Classics* (New York: Avon, 1965), pp. 146–150.

84   **"Atlanta—it was a word fitly spoken":** W. E. B. Du Bois to Booker T. Washington, September 24, 1895, in Herbert Aptheker, ed., *The Correspondence of W. E. B. Du Bois, Volume I, 1877–1934* (Amherst: University of Massachusetts Press, 1973), p. 39.

84   **"with the South in political sympathy":** W. E. B. Du Bois, *Dusk of Dawn: An Essay toward an Autobiography of a Race Concept* (New York: Harcourt, Brace, 1940), p. 55.

84   **had "recommended" him "as strongly as I could":** Booker T. Washington to W. E. B. Du Bois, March 11, 1900, in Aptheker, *Correspondence*, p. 44.

84   **"have accepted," Du Bois later admitted:** W. E. B. Du Bois, "My Evolving Program for Negro Freedom," in Rayford W. Logan, ed., *What the Negro Wants* (Chapel Hill: University of North Carolina Press, 1944), p. 54.

85   **Du Bois predicted, "will be the day of its salvation":** Francis L. Broderick, *W. E. B. Du Bois: Negro Leader in a Time of Crisis* (Stanford University Press of California, 1959), p. 66.

86   **or relied on in the struggle against Washington:** See August Meier, *Negro Thought in America, 1880–1915* (Ann Arbor: University of Michigan Press, 1963).

86   **"a number of my fugitive pieces":** Du Bois, *Dusk of Dawn*, p. 80.

87 **"by biblical and mythological narrative, metaphor and allusion":** Farah Jasmine Griffin, "Introduction," in W. E. B. Du Bois, *The Souls of Black Folk* (New York: Barnes and Noble Classics, centennial edition, 2003), pp. xvi-xviii.

88 **"themselves rather than upon the whites":** Du Bois, *Dusk of Dawn*, p. 80.

88 **as candidates for Rhodes scholarships in the Atlanta area:** Broderick, *W. E. B. Du Bois*. Broderick was a white liberal historian who, while sympathizing with the civil rights cause, nevertheless bore critical animus towards Du Bois. In his book, for example, Broderick declared that "no single work" of Du Bois, "except *The Philadelphia Negro*, is first-class." He condemned *Black Reconstruction* for "its eccentric racist-Marxist interpretations." Broderick also believed that "it seems unlikely that Du Bois will be remembered as a literary artist. . . . His reputation as a writer will rest more on the *Crisis* than on his forays into *belles lettres.*" See pp. 228–229.

89 **"in their natural state as does [Washington]":** "The Negro Question," *The New York Times*, April 24, 1903.

90 **found few readers on "its own bottom":** Broderick, *W. E. B. Du Bois*, p. 70; and Elliott M. Rudwick, *W. E. B. Du Bois, A Study in Minority Group Leadership* (Philadelphia: University of Pennsylvania Press, 1960), pp. 69–70.

90 **"teach him to obey them in English":** "Two Typical Leaders," *Outlook* (New York), vol. 73, no. 4 (May 23, 1903), pp. 214–216. The *Outlook* warned its black readers "not [to] think about your woes or your wrongs. Meditate not on 'the souls of black folk' but on 'the future of the American negro.' Look out, not in; forward, not backward. . . . Do not look long on the one-roomed cabins, or on the mortgaged farms, or the usurious rates of interest, or on the Jim Crow cars, or on the short-term schools" (p. 216).

91 **"writing realized the hopelessness of it all":** John Spencer Basset, "Two Negro Leaders," *South Atlantic Quarterly*, vol. 2, no. 3 (July 1903), pp. 267–272. Basset also observed that African Americans "are very weak human beings," and a

"child race. To give them at once the liberty of adults would debauch them" (p. 268).

91 **"he occupies. . . . The result is truly pathetic"**: "Social, Economic and Political Problems," *The American Monthly Review of Reviews,* vol. 38, no. 2 (August 1903), p. 249.

91 **"every page. It is almost intolerably sad"**: "The Souls of Black Folk" (review), *The Nation,* vol. 76, no. 1980 (June 11, 1903), pp. 481–482.

92 **"of the Negro has been a failure"**: "Behind the Veil," *Congregationalist and Christian World,* vol. 888, no. 26 (June 27, 1903), p. 912.

92 **"masters of the Anglo-Saxon race in America"**: "Politics, Economics, Sociology," *Independent* (New York), vol. 55, no. 2868 (November 19, 1903), pp. 2746–2748.

92 **"without possibility of dispute, under this category"**: "How It Feels to Be a Problem," *Outwest* (Los Angeles), vol. 19, no. 1 (July 1903), p. 93.

94 **"decay of color-prejudice might come to pass"**: "The Negro Problem," (London) *Times Literary Supplement,* no. 88 (August 14, 1903), p. 243.

94 **"your book with the same delighted appreciation"**: Ida B. Wells-Barnett to W. E. B. Du Bois, May 30, 1903, in Aptheker, *Correspondence,* pp. 54–56.

95 **"likely to see the race problem solved"**: Casely Hayford to W. E. B. Du Bois, June 8, 1904, in Aptheker, *Correspondence,* pp. 75–76.

95 **"course only *if you give* your authorization"**: Max Weber to W. E. B. Du Bois, March 30, 1905, in Aptheker, *Correspondence,* pp. 106–107.

95 **"simply because his feeling is so fine"**: Jessie Fauset to W. E. B. Du Bois, December 26, 1903, in Aptheker, *Correspondence,* p. 66.

96 **"of it and sometimes I do not"**: W. E. B. Du Bois, "The Souls of Black Folk," *Independent,* vol. 57, no. 2920 (November 17, 1904), p. 1152.

99 **"leaders and played much larger historic roles"**: See Harold R. Isaacs, *The New World of Negro Americans* (New York: John Day, 1963).

99   **acknowledged being directly influenced by Du Bois:** Gerald
       Horne, *Black and Red: W. E. B. Du Bois and the African-
       American Response to the Cold War, 1944–1963* (Albany:
       State University of New York Press, 1986), p, 315.

99   **"genius that chose to be a Communist":** Martin Luther
       King Jr., quoted in Horne, *Black and Red,* pp. 239, 5.

100   **"a hundred-year study of the Black Experience":** Vincent
       Harding, "Introduction," in Institute of the Black World,
       ed., *IBW and Education for Liberation, Black Paper No. 1*
       (Chicago: Third World Press, 1973), p. iv. In 1969, Harding
       had also observed that Du Bois "was likely the most signifi-
       cant voice to prepare the way for this current, newest stage
       of blackness. He is the proper context for an adequate un-
       derstanding of Malcolm, of Fanon, of Stokely Carmichael
       and Martin Luther King." See Vincent Harding, "W. E. B.
       Du Bois and the Black Messianic Vision," *Freedomways,*
       vol. 9 (First Quarter 1969), pp. 44–58.

100   *and Imagination of W. E. B. Du Bois* **in 1976:** See Horne,
       Black and Red; Cedric Robinson, *Black Marxism* (Chapel
       Hill: University of North Carolina Press, 1998); Cedric
       Robinson, *Black Movements in America* (New York: Rout-
       ledge, 1997); and Arnold Rampersad, *The Art and Imagina-
       tion of W. E. B. Du Bois* (Cambridge: Harvard University
       Press, 1976).

101   **future scholarship and subsequent treatments of Du Bois:**
       See, for example, Herbert Aptheker, ed., *The Correspondence
       of W. E. B. Du Bois,* three volumes (Amherst: University of
       Massachusetts Press, 1973, 1976, 1978); Aptheker, ed., *Writ-
       ings by W. E. B. Du Bois in Non-Periodical Literature Edited
       by Others* (Millwood, New York: Kraus-Thomson, 1982);
       Aptheker, ed., *Writings in Periodicals Edited by W. E. B.
       Du Bois: Selections from the "Crisis,"* two volumes (Mill-
       wood, New York: Kraus-Thomson, 1983); Aptheker, ed.,
       *Writings in Periodicals Edited by W. E. B. Du Bois: Selections
       from the "Horizon"* (Millwood, New York: Kraus-Thomson,
       1983); Aptheker, ed., *Annotated Bibliography of the Pub-
       lished Writings of W. E. B. Du Bois* (Millwood, New York:

Kraus-Thomson, 1973); and Aptheker, ed., *Writings in Peri-odicals Edited by W. E. B. Du Bois: Selections from "Phylon"* (Millwood, New York: Kraus-Thomson, 1980).

101 **"direction of peace, justice, and true internationalism"**: Sheila D. Collins, *The Rainbow Challenge: The Jackson Campaign and the Future of U.S. Politics* (New York: Monthly Review Press, 1986), pp. 145–155. Collins also noted that Jackson's 1983 address announcing his intention to compete in the Democratic presidential primaries represented "placing him-self within a historic tradition" of struggle which included Du Bois and others (p. 148).

102 **"constituencies, and its stance on foreign policy."**: Ibid., p. 155.

102 **racism had been an international calamity**: Paul Buhle, *Marxism in the United States: Remapping the History of the American Left* (London: Verso, 1987), p. 169.

103 **every aspect of civic and public life**: Angela Y. Davis, *Women, Race and Class* (New York: Random House, 1981), pp. 146–147.

103 **highly positive, with few exceptions**: Giddings does note, for example, that antilynching activist Ida B. Wells-Barnett blamed Du Bois for having her name briefly dropped from the list of founding organizers of the NAACP. Wells-Barnett also criticized Du Bois along with other "college-bred Ne-groes" for endorsing as chairman white activist Mary White Ovington as chairman of the group's executive committee. Ovington "has made little effort to know the soul of the Black Woman," Wells-Barnett bitterly declared. See Paula Giddings, *When and Where I Enter: The Impact of Black Women on Race and Sex in America* (New York: Bantam Books, 1984), pp. 180–181.

103 **"perpetuate a male-dominated literary and critical tradition"**: Mary Ellen Washington, "'The Darkened Eye Restored': Notes Toward a Literary History of Black Women," in Henry Louis Gates Jr., ed., *Reading Black Reading Feminist: A Criti-cal Anthology* (New York: Meridian/New American Library, 1990), p. 33.

104 **"of just what that term might mean"**: Nellie Y. McKay, "The Souls of Black Women Folk in the Writings of W. E. B. Du Bois," in Gates, *Reading Black Reading Feminist,* pp. 227–243.

105 **"important for young women as for young men"**: Shirley Wilson Logan, *"We Are Coming": The Persuasive Discourse of Nineteenth Century Black Women* (Carbondale and Edwardsville: Southern Illinois University Press, 1999), pp. 157–158.

106 **childhood, teenage years, and early adulthood:** See *Washington Post,* December 13, 1993, quoted in David J. Garrow, review of David Levering Lewis, *W. E. B. Du Bois: A Biography of a Race, 1868–1919* (New York: Henry Holt and Company, 1993), in *Journal of American History,* vol. 81, no. 2 (September 1994), pp. 620–622.

107 **"about the failure of the American dream"**: To his credit, however, Julian Bond also admitted that Du Bois did not always adhere to the liberal integrationist creed. Bond noted: "Absolute consistency was never Du Bois's strong point. He never blindly followed the path he had prescribed without some deviation." See Julian Bond, "Foreword," in Arthur J. Magida, *Prophet of Rage: A Life of Louis Farrakhan and His Nation* (New York: Basic Books, 1996), pp. x-xi.

108 **"authoritarian power, particularly if it is anti-American"**: Gerald Early, review of David Levering Lewis, *W. E. B. Du Bois: The Fight for Equality and the American Century, 1919–1963* (New York: Henry Holt and Company, 2000), in *National Review,* vol. 52, no. 23 (December 4, 2000), pp. 58–62.

109 **"seem politically foolish and even morally abhorrent"**: Alan Brinkley, "Autumn of the Agitator," *New Republic,* vol. 224, nos. 1–2 (January 1, 2001), pp. 26–30. Like Lewis, Brinkley interpreted Du Bois' exile in Ghana as a tragic culmination of his alliance with "the far left": "[As] if to confirm his final alienation from his own nation, [Du Bois] left the United States for Ghana, where he became the revered ward of the leftist regime of Kwame Nkrumah. He died there in August 1963, on the eve of the great March on Washington that

marked a culmination of many of Du Bois's early dreams but that now seemed to him a largely irrelevant gesture against a world incapable of granting equality to people of color without revolutionary change."

110 **"the status of Africans in the world"**: V. P. Franklin, review of Lewis, *W. E. B. Du Bois: The Fight for Equality,* in *Journal of American History,* vol. 89, no. 1 (June 2002), pp. 189–191.

110 **"choices Du Bois made throughout his public career"**: Judith Stein, "The Difficult Doctor Du Bois," *Reviews in American History,* vol. 29, no. 2 (2001), pp. 247–254. Philosopher Joseph DeMarco, author of an excellent book on Du Bois, makes the same point about Lewis's inability to address the theoretical and philosophical groundings Du Bois held, which, in turn, informed his political and tactical decisions. "Following Du Bois's reasoning requires a different book," DeMarco argued. "Without it, as is the case with *The Fight for Equality,* [Du Bois's] change in emphasis, for those who want an explanation, can be perceived as random." See Joseph DeMarco, review of Lewis, *W. E. B. Du Bois: The Fight for Equality* in *New England Quarterly,* vol. 74, no. 3 (September 2001), pp. 514–515.

111 **"to be testified and fought against courageously"**: Edward W. Said, *Representation of the Intellectual* (New York: Vintage Books, 1994), pp. 11–12.

113 **"anti-colonialism and they openly showed their respect"**: Horne, *Black and Red,* p. 287.

115 **"(in the end he remains a liberal)"**: E. Franklin Frazier, "The Du Bois Program in the Present Crisis," *Race: Devoted to Social, Political, and Economic Equality,* vol. 1, no. 1 (Winter 1935–1936), pp. 11–13.

115 **"encouragement of future economic and race war"**: W. E. B. Du Bois, "The Future of Europe in Africa," in Aptheker, ed., *Against Racism,* pp. 173–184.

116 **"thought and not freedom for private profit-making"**: W. E. B. Du Bois, "The Future of Europe in Africa," in Aptheker, ed., *Against Racism,* pp. 184–198. Du Bois provocatively added: "For this reason, the colonial and quasi-colonial peoples will be more ready to achieve and accept

this Democracy of industry, than the misled people of Europe whose conception of democracy has been industrial anarchy with the spirit of man in chains."

117 novel, *The Quest of the Silver Fleece*: W. E. B. Du Bois, *The Quest of the Silver Fleece: A Novel* (Chicago: A. C. McClurg, 1911).

117 writing *Dark Princess: A Romance* in 1928: W. E. B. Du Bois, *Dark Princess: A Romance* (New York: Harcourt, Brace, 1928).

117 *Builds a School,* and *Worlds of Color*: W. E. B. Du Bois, *The Ordeal of Mansart* (New York: Mainstream, 1957); Du Bois, *Mansart Builds a School* (New York, Mainstream, 1959); and Du Bois, *Worlds of Color* (New York: Mainstream, 1961).

118 World War I, and in Los Angeles in 1924: Du Bois, *The Autobiography of W. E. B. Du Bois* (New York: International Publishers, 1968), p. 270.

118 *"practical activity* of the proletariat is necessary": Perry Anderson, *Considerations on Western Marxism* (London: Verso, 1979), p. 105.

Chapter 4

121 "sleep /Every goodbye ain't gone." Lewis Micheaux, quoted in James Harley and Keith Moore, "Malcolm X: The Mystery, Legacy of Death Remain," (New York) *Daily News,* February 21, 1985.

123 "against all forms of discrimination": Ilyasah Shabazz, Gamilah Shabazz, and Malaak Shabazz to Manning Marable, undated letter regarding the opening of the "Malcolm X and Dr. Betty Shabazz Memorial and Educational Center, Inc.," May 2005.

123 "as a friend, swell": Felicia R. Lee, "Malcolm X the Thinker, Brought into Focus," *New York Times,* May 14, 2005.

124 Malcolm X and Dr. Betty Shabazz Memorial Center formal opening: www.columbia.edu/cu/news/05/05/malcolm.html.

124 **"the difficulties of Malcolm's quest"**: Edward Rothstein, "The Personal Evolution of a Civil Rights Giant," *New York Times,* May 19, 2005.

124 **"reluctant to draw too many distinctions"**: Ibid.

126 **the sale and destruction of the Audubon**: "Columbia is Buying Audubon Ballroom; Demolition Planned," *New York Times,* February 24, 1983.

126 **"Columbia is purchasing Malcolm's tomb!"**: AFRAM news reprint, Harlem, New York, March 1, 1983.

126 **the commercial viability of the community**: Peggy Dye, "High Tech Ballroom," *Village Voice,* December 5, 1989.

127 **"whose medicines they cannot afford"**: Ibid.

129 **popular resistance to Columbia's gentrification plans**: Peggy Dye, "Fight Goes On for Audubon," *New York Times,* January 3, 1991.

130 **by the neighborhood's economic transformation:** An excellent examination of the economic effects of Harlem's gentrification since 1990 is Derek G. Hyra's "Racial Uplift? Intra-Racial Class Conflict and the Economic Revitalization of Harlem and Bronzeville," presented at the Fall 2004 W. E. B. Du Bois Institute for African and African American Research Colloquium Series, Harvard University, November 17, 2004. In this research, Hyra finds that the percentage of Central Harlem's population with a BA degree also increased by 50 percent from 1990 to 2000, and the percentage of neighborhood homeowners jumped by 65 percent. These striking socioeconomic changes, according to Hyra, have increasingly marginalized Harlem's poor residents.

130 **originally developed by geographer David Harvey:** See Leith Mullings, "Interrogating Racism: Toward an Anti-Racist Anthropology," *Annual Review of Anthropology,* vol. 34 (2005); also see David Harvey, *The New Imperialism* (New York: Oxford University Press, 2003).

130 **accumulation of profits for new black elites:** See Mary Pattillo, "Negotiating Blackness, For Richer or For Poorer," *Ethnography,* vol. 4, no. 1 (2003), pp. 61–93; and Mary

Pattillo-McCoy, *Black Picket Fences* (Chicago: University of Chicago Press, 1999).

132 **spirit and legacy of Malcolm X?:** Ilyasah Shabazz, Gamilah Shabazz, and Malaak Shabazz to Manning Marable, May 2005.

133 **"Daddy was! All these ridiculous clichés":** Ellen Hopkins, "Their Father's Daughters," *Rolling Stone,* November 30, 1989, p. 124.

135 **almost treasonous to the entire black race:** Immediately following Malcolm X's assassination, several individuals who had worked closely with the fallen leader sought to document his meaning to the larger black freedom struggle. These early texts include: Leslie Alexander Lacy, "Malcolm X in Ghana," in John Henrik Clarke, ed., *Malcolm X: The Man and His Times* (New York: Macmillan, 1969), pp. 217–255; Ossie Davis, "Why I Eulogized Malcolm X," *Negro Digest,* vol. 15, no. 4 (February 1966), pp. 64–66; Wyatt Tee Walker, "On Malcolm X: Nothing But a Man," *Negro Digest,* vol. 14, no. 10 (August 1965), pp. 29–32; and Albert B. Cleage Jr., "Brother Malcolm," in Cleage, *The Black Messiah* (New York: Sheed and Ward, 1968), pp. 186–200. The advocates of Black Power subsequently placed Malcolm X firmly within the black nationalist tradition of Martin R. Delany and Marcus Garvey, emphasizing his dedication to the use of armed self-defense by blacks. Amiri Baraka's essay, "The Legacy of Malcolm X, and the Coming of the Black Nation," in LeRoi Jones, *Home: Social Essays* (New York: William Morrow, 1966), pp. 238–250, became the template for this line of interpretation. Following Baraka's black nationalist thesis were: Eldridge Cleaver, "Initial Reactions on the Assassination of Malcolm X," in Cleaver, *Soul on Ice* (New York: Ramparts, 1968), pp. 50–61; James Boggs, "King, Malcolm, and the Future of the Black Revolution," in Boggs, *Racism and the Class Struggle: Further Pages from a Black Worker's Notebook* (New York: Monthly Review Press, 1970), pp. 104–129; Cedric Robinson, "Malcolm Little as a Charismatic Leader,"

Afro-American Studies, vol. 2, no. 1 (September 1972), pp. 81–96; and Robert Allen, *Black Awakening in Capitalist America* (Garden City, N.Y.: Anchor/Doubleday, 1970), especially pp. 30–40.

138 **"and pushing us to walls"**: Gwendolyn Brooks, "Malcolm X," in James B. Gwynne, ed., *Malcolm X: A Tribute* (New York: Steppingstones Press, 1983), p. 13.

138 **"floods the womb until I drown"**: Sonia Sanchez, "Malcolm," in Gwynne, *Malcolm X: A Tribute*, p. 16.

140 **"faggots till the end of the earth"**: Amiri Baraka, "A Poem for Black Hearts," in Dudley Randall and Margaret G. Burroughs, eds., *For Malcolm: Poems on the Life and Death of Malcolm X* (Detroit: Broadside Press, 1967), pp. 61–62. An excellent discussion of Malcolm X's influence as the archetypal masculinist figure within African-American culture is in Maria Josefina Saldana-Portillo, "Consuming Malcolm X: Prophecy and Performative Masculinity," *Novel: A Forum on Fiction*, vol. 30, no. 3 (Spring 1997), pp. 289–308.

141 **the provocative phrase, "Too Black, Too Strong"**: Public Enemy, *It Takes a Nation of Millions to Hold Us Back*, DefJam Recordings, 1988.

141 **a secure and empowering black male figure**: Michael Eric Dyson, *Making Malcolm: The Myth and Meaning of Malcolm X* (New York: Oxford University Press, 1995).

142 **"like Malcolm ready to bring that noise"**: Ice Cube, *The Predator*, Priority Records P2–57198, 1992.

142 **"to beat my ass if I don't go pop?"**: Makaveli [Tupac Shakur], *Don Killuminati: The 7 Day Theory*, Death Row INTD–90039, 1996.

142 **"smacked, turn the other cheek"**: Tupac Shakur, "Words of Wisdom," *2Pacalypse Now*, Interscope P2 50603, 1991.

143 **"get me high as trapeze"**: AZ the Visualiza, "Rather Unique," *Doe or Die*, EMI E2–32631, 1995.

143 **"but we picked it together"**: Heavy D and the Boyz, "Letter to the Future," *Peaceful Journey*, MCA/Uptown MCAD 10289, 1991.

144 **"word does nothing against the feds"**: The Fugees, "Beast," *The Score,* Ruff House/Columbia CK 67147, 1996.

144 **"while the rich profit off our blood?"**: Ani DiFranco, "To the Teeth," *To the Teeth,* Righteous Babe Records RBR017, 1999.

145 **"as opposed to dramatic entertainment"**: Bernard Weinraub, "Hollywood Totals Up a Holiday Season of Mixed Blessings," *New York Times,* January 4, 1993, p. C11.

145 **by "Malcolm X the product"**: Thomas Doherty, "Malcolm X: In Print, on Screen," *Biography,* vol. 23, no. 1 (2000), pp. 29–48.

145 **X-related products at $100 million in 1992:** Tonya Pendleton, "The Mainstreaming of Malcolm X: How much control does Spike Lee have?" *Philadelphia Tribune,* November 17, 1992. Also see Johnnie L. Roberts "Movies: Selling, 'Malcolm X' Successfully Means Pulling a White Audience," *Wall Street Journal,* November 16, 1992.

147 **"finally as America's stamp of approval"**: Ossie Davis, interview by author, July 29, 2003.

147 **"disavowed his earlier separatist preaching"**: See Marion Davis, "Black History Month Stamp Ceremony Will Celebrate Malcolm X," *The Providence Journal-Bulletin* (Providence, R.I.), February 19, 1999, p. 1B.

149 **"such a potent, racist cult," Haley's article concluded:** Alex Haley, "Mr. Muhammad Speaks," *Reader's Digest,* March 1960.

150 **"among the Negro people are also exaggerated"**: M. A. Jones to Mr. DeLoach, FBI Memorandum, October 9, 1962, in Anne Romaine Collection, Box 1, University of Tennessee Library Special Collection, Knoxville, Tennessee. Balk agreed "to treat the threat posed by the NOI in a realistic and accurate manner." The FBI agent stipulated that any data provided to Haley and Balk would not be attributed" to the bureau.

151 **"will the field be left to extremists?"**: Alfred Balk and Alex Haley, "Black Merchants of Hate," *Saturday Evening Post,* vol. 236, no. 3, January 26, 1963, pp. 67–74.

151   "thereby carry out our [the FBI's] investigative responsibilities": M. A. Jones to Mr. DeLoach, February 6, 1963, in Anne Romaine Collection, Box 1.

152   "the leadership [of the NOI] if he wants it": Balk and Haley, "Black Merchants of Hate," p. 74.

152   were going "downhill" before their deaths: In an extraordinary interview with writer Thomas Hauser, Alex Haley stated that he had "worked closely with Malcolm X." Haley said, "I also did a *Playboy* interview with Martin Luther King during the same period, so I knew one very closely and the other a little." Based on his knowledge of both men, he had concluded that they had "both died tragically at about the right time in terms of posterity. Both men were . . . beginning to decline. They were under attack." In Haley's opinion, Malcolm, in particular, "was having a rough time trying to keep things going. Both of them were killed just before it went really downhill for them, and as of their death, they were practically sainted." See Thomas Hauser, *Muhammad Ali: His Life and Times* (New York: Touchstone/Simon and Schuster, 1991), p. 508.

154   Washington's 1901 memoir, *Up from Slavery*: See Booker T. Washington, *Up from Slavery* (Garden City, NY: Doubleday & Co., 1901).

156   "some of it rather lava-like": On January 9, 1964, Haley wrote to Doubleday Executive Editor Kenneth McCormick and his agent, Paul Reynolds, that "the most impact material of the book, some of it rather lava-like, is what I have from Malcolm for the three essay chapters, 'The Negro,' 'The End of Christianity,' and 'Twenty Million Black Muslims.'" See Alex Haley to Kenneth McCormick, Wolcott Gibbs Jr., and Paul Reynolds, January 19, 1964, in Anne Romaine Collection.

158   cost the publisher millions of dollars: In early March 1965, Doubleday's senior management voted not to publish *The Autobiography of Malcolm X*, over editor Kenneth McCormick's vigorous objections. McCormick informed Haley on

March 16 that "the hardest thing I ever had to do" was to grant permission to Haley's agent, Paul Reynolds, "to show [the book manuscript] to other publishers." Doubleday had already paid Malcolm X and Haley $13,750 as of February 1965, but agreed to be repaid $10,000 from a pending contract by Grove Press to settle the debt. See Kenneth McCormick to Alex Haley, March 16, 1965; Alex Haley to Kenneth McCormick, March 22, 1965; Kenneth McCormick to Bob Banker, April 7, 1965; and Malcolm Reiss to Kenneth McCormick, April 21, 1965, in the Kenneth McCormick Collection of the Records of Doubleday & Co., Manuscript Division, Library of Congress Series: Publishing Case Files, Box 44.

158   **had begun well *prior* to his assassination:** See the correspondence of Alex Haley to Kenneth McCormick in the Kenneth McCormick Collection. In the early 1960s the Nation of Islam had been directly involved with the American Nazi Party and white supremacist organizations—all while Malcolm X had been its "national representative." This regrettable dimension of Malcolm's career had to be thoroughly investigated, yet few scholars, black or white, had been willing to do so.

159   **"to change any material you still deem libelous":** Ibid.

161   **listed the *Autobiography* in the top ten:** Paul Gray, "Required Reading," *Time,* June 8, 1998, p. 105.

161   **scholarly papers over the years:** On Malcolm X's skillful use of language and rhetoric, see Robert E. Terrill, "Colonizing the Borderlands: Shifting Circumference in the Rhetoric of Malcolm X," *Quarterly Journal of Speech,* vol. 86, no. 1 (February 2000), pp. 67–85.

163   **objective appraisal of him or his legacy:** The best available studies of Malcolm X merit some consideration here. Although originally written more than three decades ago, *Newsweek* editor/journalist Peter Goldman's *The Death and Life of Malcolm X* (New York: Harper and Row, 1973) still remains an excellent introduction to the man and his times. Well written and researched, Goldman's text is based on his own interviews with the subject. Karl Evanzz's *The Judas Fac-*

tor: The Plot to Kill Malcolm X (New York: Thunder's Mouth Press, 1992) presents a persuasive argument explaining the FBI's near-blanket surveillance of the subject. Evanzz suggests that NOI National Secretary John Ali may have been an FBI informant. Louis A. DeCaro Jr. has written two thoughtful studies on Malcolm X's spiritual growth and religious orientation: *On the Side of My People: A Religious Life of Malcolm X* (New York: New York University Press, 1996); and *Malcolm and the Cross: The Nation of Islam, Malcolm X and Christianity* (New York: New York University Press, 1998). DeCaro graciously agreed to be interviewed in 2001 for the Malcolm X Project at Columbia.

The field of religious studies has produced other informative interpretations of Malcolm X. These works include: Lewis V. Baldwin, *Between Cross and Crescent: Christian and Muslim Perspectives on Malcolm and Martin* (Gainesville: University of Florida, 2002); a sound recording by Hamam Cross, Donna Scott, and Eugene Seals, "What's Up with Malcolm? The Real Failure of Islam" (Southfield, Michigan: Readings for the Blind, 2001); and Peter J. Paris, *Black Religious Leaders: Conflict in Unity* (Westminster: John Knox Press, 1991).

164 **unfamiliar with what the man** *actually said***:** George Breitman, ed., *Malcolm X Speaks* (New York: Merit Publishers, 1965); and George Breitman, ed., *By Any Means Necessary* (New York: Pathfinder Press, 1970).

164 **value of $300–$400, sold for nearly $6,000:** "'Gatsby,' 'Malcolm X' Big Stars at Auction," Associated Press wire story, March 14, 1993.

165 **was able to block the sale:** See William Bastone, "FBI Probes Purloined Files," *Village Voice,* July 27, 1999; "Court Clerk Arrested and Charged in the Malcolm Diary," *Jet* magazine, vol. 97, no. 6 (January 17, 2000), p. 48; and Diego Ribadeneira, "Missing Malcolm X Diary Up for Auction in California," *Boston Globe,* May 18, 1999.

166 **should have made the sale null and void:** The best accounts of the theft, abortive auction, and subsequent recovery of the

Malcolm X memorabilia are provided in Thulani Davis, "What Becomes a Legend Most?" *Village Voice* April 9, 2002; Kendra Hamilton, "Malcolm X Archival Material Rescued from the Auction Block," *Black Issues in Higher Education,* vol. 19, no. 4 (April 11, 2002), pp. 62–63; and Lynne Duke, "A Bid to Preserve the Papers of Malcolm X; Scuttled Auction Highlights Chaos in Leader's Estate," *Washington Post,* March 20, 2002.

169 **"private party sale for the entire collection":** Emily Eakin, "Auction House Withdraws Items Attributed to Malcolm X," *New York Times,* March 13, 2002; and Debra Kong, "Auction House Cancels Malcolm X Sale," Associated Press wire story, March 13, 2002.

170 **"Malcolm X ever to hit the market":** Moments in Time, www.momentsintime.com/Malcolm%20X.htm.

170 **"would fetch a similar sum":** Sholto Byrnes, "Pandora," *Independent,* June 5, 2002, p. 24.

171 **"with his wife's sexual demands":** "Malcolm X's Sexual Suffering," *New York Post,* June 4, 2002, p. 10.

172 **"wives, or their women":** Malcolm X with Alex Haley, *The Autobiography of Malcolm X* (New York: Ballantine Books, 1992), p. 206.

172 **"he was a married man!":** Louis Farrakhan, interview by author, May 9, 2005.

173 **"heard hints" about Muhammad's serial adultery:** Malcolm X with Alex Haley, *The Autobiography of Malcolm X,* p. 301.

174 **"Where he leads, I will follow":** Ibid., p. 457.

174 **tragedy and triumph of the moment:** Ibid., p. 461. The funeral oration given by Davis was a brilliant defense of the lasting significance of Malcolm X to the Harlem community and to the African-American people, but it also portrayed him as masculinist and patriarchal. For Davis, "Malcolm was our manhood, our living, black manhood! That was his meaning to his people. And, in honoring him, we honor the best in ourselves. . . . And we will know him then for what he

was and is—a Prince—our own black shining Prince!—who
didn't hesitate to die, because he loved us so" (p. 462).

174   **short, his potential unfulfilled:** Ossie Davis, interview by author, July 29, 2003.

175   **"to get rid of him":** C. L. R. James, "Black Power," lecture,
London, 1967, in Anna Grimshaw, ed., *The C. L. R. James
Reader* (Oxford: Blackwell Publishers, 1992), pp. 362–374.

176   **"why you want me to die homie?":** 50 Cent (featuring Lloyd
Banks), "Many Men (Wish Death)," *Get Rich or Die Tryin',*
Shady/Aftermath/Interscope 0694935442, 2003.

Chapter 5

179   **Bob Marley, "War":** Bob Marley and the Wailers, "War,"
Rastaman Vibration, Island Records, 1976. Marley set to
music words from an address by Haile Selassie of Ethiopia,
delivered before the United Nations, October 4, 1963.

182   **"to the case being presented":** Robert L. Carter, *A Matter of
Law: A Memoir of Struggle in the Cause of Equal Rights*
(New York: New Press, 2005), p. 62.

183   **"the desire to study law":** Ibid., p. 78.

184   **"the facts will set you free":** Ibid., p. 87.

184   **challenge the legitimacy of Jim Crow segregation:** Ibid.,
p. 126.

185   **legal argument to outlaw separate schools:** See Kenneth
Clark, "The Development of Consciousness of Self and
the Emergence of Racial Identity in Negro Preschool
Children," *Journal of Social Psychology,* vol. 10 (1939),
pp. 591–599.

185   **"Separate educational facilities are inherently unequal":**
Juan Williams, *Eyes on the Prize: America's Civil Rights
Years, 1954–1965* (New York: Penguin, 1987), p. 34. In re-
sponding to *Brown,* the *Washington Post* declared editori-
ally: "It is not too much to speak of the Court's decision as
a new birth of freedom. It comes at a juncture in the affairs
of mankind when this reaffirmation of basic human values

is likely to have a wonderfully tonic effect. America is rid of an incubus which impeded and embarrassed it in all its relations with the world" (p. 35).

186   **"be given meaning at home"**: See Derrick Bell, "*Brown* and the Interest-Convergence Dilemma," in Derrick Bell, ed., *Shades of Brown* (New York: Teachers College Press, 1980), pp. 90–106.

186   **"to us to lure white voters"**: Carter, *A Matter of Law*, pp. 185–186.

191   **up to 341,000 by 1975**: See table 70, "Level of Schooling Completed for Persons 25 and Over," and table 71, "Selected Levels of Schooling Completed for Persons 25 to 34," in Bureau of the Census, *The Social and Economic Status of the Black Population in the United States: An Historical View, 1790–1978* (Washington, D.C.: U.S. Government Printing Office, 1980), pp. 93–94.

191   **for them to attend college**: See Manning Marable, *How Capitalism Underdeveloped Black America* (Boston: South End Press, 1983), p. 218.

192   **"which we upheld in *Brown*."** See Leland Ware, "The Unfulfilled Promise," *Crisis*, vol. 111, no. 3 (May/June 2004), pp. 40–42.

193   **"same Constitution stands as a barrier"**: Thurgood Marshall quoted in Charles J. Ogletree Jr., *All Deliberate Speed* (New York: W. W. Norton, 2004), pp. 160–161.

193   **24 percent, in only ten years**: See "Occupations of Black Workers, 14 Years Old and Over, 1940, 1960, 1970," in Bureau of the Census, *The Social and Economic Status of the Black Population*, p. 74.

195   **"the academy to its center"**: Peter Applebaum, "Can Harvard's Powerhouse Alter the Course of Black Studies?" *New York Times*, November 3, 1996.

196   **with 1,656 new doctorates produced in 2000**: Marable, *The Great Wells of Democracy*, pp. 141–142.

197   **prepared for these new higher educational opportunities**: Ware, "The Unfulfilled Promise," p. 42.

199   **"middle class or upper middle class"**: William G. Bowen and Derek Bok, quoted in Richard D. Kahlenberg, "Toward Affirmative Action for Economic Diversity," *Chronicle of Higher Education*, vol. 50, no. 28 (March 19, 2004), p. B12.

199   **all students at these elite institutions**: Mary Beth Marklein, "The wealth gap on campus: Low-income students scarce at elite collectes," *USFL Today*, September 30, 2004.

199   **number drops to 20 percent**: Joni Finney and Kristin Conklin, "Enough of Trickle Down: It's Time for a Flood of Aid for Needy Students," *Chronicle of Higher Education*, vol. 46, no. 35 (May 5, 2000), p. A68.

200   **preserving the hierarchy of white elite privilege**: See Daniel Golden, "At Many Colleges the Rich Kids Get Affirmative Action," *Wall Street Journal*, February 20, 2003.

201   **"is to disregard its virtues"**: See George Derek Musgrove, "Good at the Game of Tricknology: Proposition 209 and the Struggle for the Historical Memory of the Civil Rights Movement," *Souls*, vol. 1, no. 3 (Summer 1999), pp. 7–24.

201   **"affirmative action has been around"**: William Clinton quoted in Marable, *The Great Wells of Democracy*, p. 81.

202   **followed California in outlawing affirmative action enforcement**: "Do Blacks Still Get an Admissions Advantage at the Elite Campuses of the University of California?" *Journal of Blacks in Higher Education*, no. 41 (Winter 2003/2004), pp. 38–39.

203   **down to 10.8 percent in 2001**: Sara Hebel, "'Percent Plans' Don't Add Up," *Chronicle of Higher Education*, vol. 49, no. 28 (March 21, 2003), pp. A22-A26.

204   **to maintain such preferences was unconstitutional**: Peter Schmidt, "Bush Briefs in Michigan Cases Leave Little Room to Use Race in Admissions," *Chronicle of Higher Education*, vol. 49, no. 21 (January 31, 2003), pp. A23–A24.

205   **"before the court's respite ends"**: Curt A. Levey, "Colleges Should Take No Comfort in the Supreme Court's Reprieve," *Chronicle of Higher Education*, vol. 49, no. 45 (July 18, 2003), pp. B11-B12.

205 **"in limiting the use of preferences"**: Roger Clegg, "Time Has Not Favored Racial Preferences," *Chronicle of Higher Education*, vol. 51, no. 19 (January 14, 2005), pp. B10-B11.

207 **years, all in the name of "diversity"**: See Jeffrey Selingo, "Michigan: Who Really Won?" *Chronicle of Higher Education*, vol. 51, no. 19 (January 19, 2005), pp. A21-A23. At the University of Michigan at Ann Arbor, for example, the 2002 freshman class had 8.5 percent black and 5.9 percent Latino students in the matriculating class. After *Grutter v. Bollinger*, the 2004 entering class looked dramatically different: African-American students comprised only 5.8 percent, and Latinos 4.4 percent of all freshmen.

207 **were not native-born African Americans:** See Sara Rimer and Karen W. Arenson, "Top Colleges Take More Blacks, But Which Ones?" *New York Times*, June 24, 2004.

209 **actually have a negative net wealth:** See Melvin Oliver and Thomas Shapiro, *Black Wealth/White Wealth: A New Perspective on Racial Inequality* (New York: Routledge, 1995); and Thomas Shapiro, *Hidden Cost of Being African American: How Wealth Perpetuates Inequality* (New York: Oxford University Press, 2004).

209 **under $5,000 in total financial assets:** See William G. Gale and Stacie Carney, "Asset Accumulation Among Low-Income Households," The Brookings Institution, Economic Studies Paper, November 1999, available at www.brookings.edu.

210 **Denver, Houston, San Francisco, and Pittsburgh:** Ware, "The Unfulfilled Promise," pp. 40–43; and John Logan, "Resegregation in American Public Schools?" Lewis Mumford Center, April 26, 2004, available at www.mumford.albany.edu/census/report.html.

215 **were outside of the paid labor force:** Mark Levitan, "Poverty in New York City, 2004; Recovery?" A Community Service Society Annual Report, September 2004, available at www.cssny.org/index.html; and Janny Scott, "Nearly Half of Black Men Found Jobless," *New York Times*, February 28, 2004.

216 **from deli clerks to telemarketers:** Paul von Zielbauer, "Study Shows More Job Offers for Ex-Convicts Who Are White," *New York Times*, June 17, 2005.

216   unemployment starts all over again: See Marc Mauer, *Race to Incarcerate* (New York, New Press, 1999); and Angela Y. Davis, *Are Prisons Obsolete?* (New York: Seven Stories Press, 2003).

218   expense of urban, heavily minority districts: Peter Wagner, "Skewing Democracy: Where the Census Counts Prisoners," *Poverty and Race*, vol. 14, no. 2 (March/April 2005), pp. 3–4.

219   historic struggles of the Civil Rights movement: See Yolanda Rodriguez, "Immigrants Ride for Rights," *Atlanta Journal-Constitution*, September 30, 2003; Stacy A. Teicher, "Goal of new 'freedom ride': integrate illegal immigrants," *Christian Science Monitor*, October 2, 2003; and Kristin Tillotson, "Immigrants: The New Activists," *Star Tribune* (Minneapolis), April 18, 2004.

220   two universities under its authority: See Beth McMurtrie, "The Quota Quandary," and Marion Lloyd, "In Brazil, A New Debate over Color," *Chronicle of Higher Education*, vol. 50, no. 23 (February 13, 2004), pp. 36–38.

221   "conflict with a powerful competing white interest": Carter, *A Matter of Law*, p. 131.

221   "committed to fulfilling its promise": Ibid., p. 242.

Index

"A Defense of the Negro Race"
(Crummell), 48–49
democracy
African-American struggle for justice
and, 63–64
disfranchisement of blacks and, 115
Du Bois's call for democratization
of Carribean and Latin
America, 115
Du Bois's call for democratization of
colonial Africa, 116
exclusion of African Americans from
participation in, 50
impact of black freedom struggle
on, 24
racial foundation of U.S.
democracy, 15
Democratic Party
integrationists supporting, 213
racial exclusion of African Americans
and, 45
desegregation. *See* segregation
Detroit Red, 136, 143, 146. *See also*
Malcolm X
Diallo, Amadou, 6
DiFranco, Ani, 144
Dinkins, David, 127–128
disfranchisement
of black electorate in 1890s, 82–83
democracy and, 115
political economy of racialized
domination and, 215–217
dispossession through accumulation
applied to legacy of Malcolm X, 132
racism and, 130–131
diversity
Columbia programs promoting,
207–208
in corporations, 195
Grutter v. Bollinger, 204–205
obscuring racial history and present
reality of blacks, 209
percentage plans, 202
documentaries, lives of ex-slaves, 26–28
documents, lack of records of black
history, 22
Dodson, Howard, 123, 168
Doherty, Thomas, 145

Douglass, Frederick
Black Heritage Series of postage
stamps honoring, 147
Fourth of July speech, 42–43
integration politics of, 48
Dred Scott v. Sanford, 44
drug use, Malcolm X and Martin Luther
King Jr. opposition to, 133
Du Bois, David Graham, 75
Du Bois, Nina Gomer, 104
Du Bois, W. E. B., 147
academic/intellectual response to
The Souls of Black Folk,
94–95
anniversary celebration honoring,
68–72
black feminism and, 103–105
"color line" in writings of, 76
controversy regarding disagreement
with Booker T. Washington, 89–92
double consciousness of African
Americans, 76–78
dramatic pageant written by, 118
education of, 80–81
exile from U.S., 77
Farrakhan compared with, 107
Gates on influence of, 75
global view of racism, 113
ideological and political relationship
with Booker T. Washington,
85–86, 88–89, 93–94
influence on black freedom
movement, 99
as an intellectual, 111
intellectual legacy in African-American
studies, 99–101
Lewis's biography of, 105–107
Lewis's criticisms of, 108–110
McLaurin v. Oklahoma State Regent,
183–184
on Nat Turner rebellion, 4–5
on national identity of African
Americans, 52
novels of, 117
The Philadelphia Negro, 81
racial justice and, 97
reacting to response to *The Souls of
Black Folk*, 93, 95–96